$ 12.75

Principles of
Gene Manipulation

AN INTRODUCTION TO
GENETIC ENGINEERING

Studies in Microbiology

EDITORS

N. G. CARR
Department of Biochemistry
University of Liverpool

J. L. INGRAHAM
Department of Bacteriology
University of California
at Davis

S. C. RITTENBERG
Department of Bacteriology
University of California
at Los Angeles

Studies in Microbiology Volume 2

Principles of Gene Manipulation

AN INTRODUCTION TO GENETIC ENGINEERING

R. W. OLD
MA, PhD

S. B. PRIMROSE
BSc, PhD

Both at Department of Biological Sciences,
University of Warwick,
Coventry CV4 7AL, U.K.

UNIVERSITY OF CALIFORNIA PRESS

BERKELEY AND LOS ANGELES 1980

UNIVERSITY OF
CALIFORNIA PRESS
Berkeley and Los Angeles, California

**Library of Congress
Cataloging in Publication Data**

Old, R W
  Principles of gene manipulation.

  Includes index.
  1. Genetic engineering. I. Primrose, S B,
joint author. II. Title.
OH442.042   575.1   79-25736

Printed in Great Britain

Contents

Preface

Advances in biology continue to be made at a striking and ever increasing rate. One of the pace-setters is the subject matter of this book, *gene manipulation,* often popularly referred to as *genetic engineering.* A consequence of the phenomenal rate of progress in this subject has been that many biologists have found it impossible to keep pace with current developments, a situation exacerbated by the free use of jargon, and as with all rapidly growing fields it will be some time before comprehensive texts catch up. We have written this book to fill the resultant vacuum.

In the present state of the art, basic techniques are at the point of becoming well established and the trend is towards applying them to solve particular problems. Thus we have endeavoured to give readers enough details of these basic techniques to enable them to follow the current literature and future developments. In using this approach we hope that the content of the book does not date too quickly, but that the principles explained herein will provide an introduction to gene manipulation for some time to come.

The book is based on a series of twenty lectures on gene manipulation given at the University of Warwick to students on biology, microbiology and biochemistry degree courses. It is intended as an introduction to the subject for advanced undergraduates or people already in biological research, and consequently we have assumed that the reader has some prior knowledge of basic molecular biology. The literature has been surveyed up to the end of June 1979. The references cited are intended to point the reader towards the mainstream of the subject and to attribute original results to researchers. However, in a book of this size it is impossible to detail every paper. We have chosen examples from the literature which we feel best illustrate particular topics and hope that we have not offended colleagues whose experiments have not been mentioned.

Finally, it is a pleasure to acknowledge the skilled assistance of Mrs Debbie Bowns and Miss Dianne Simpson who had to interpret our sometimes impenetrable handwriting in producing the typescript; and Malcolm Davies for compiling and checking all the references.

R. W. Old
S. B. Primrose

August, 1979

Abbreviations and Conversion Scale

amber (mutation) = *am*
dihydrofolate reductase = DHFR
gene for DNA ligase = *lig*
kilobases = Kb
megadaltons = Mdal.
molecular weight = mol.wt.
plaque-forming unit = pfu
temperature-sensitive (mutation) = *ts*

Scale for conversion between Kilobase pairs of duplex DNA and molecular weight.

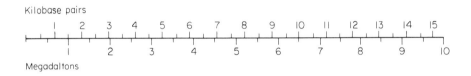

Chapter 1. Introduction

INTRODUCTION

The phrase 'gene manipulation' means different things to different people. Some, for example, would consider the sophisticated genetic manipulations undertaken daily by *Escherichia coli* geneticists as genetic manipulation. Most people, however, consider gene manipulation in a much broader context. In fact, in most Western countries there is a precise *legal* definition of gene manipulation as a result of Government legislation to control it (see Chapter 10). In the United Kingdom gene manipulation is defined as 'the formation of new combinations of heritable material by the insertion of nucleic acid molecules, produced by whatever means outside the cell, into any virus, bacterial plasmid or other vector system so as to allow their incorporation into a host organism in which they do not naturally occur but in which they are capable of continued propagation'.

The definitions adopted by other countries are similar and all adequately describe the subject matter of this book. However, in order to fully understand this definition it is necessary to consider the early development of the subject.

The Early Experiments

Some bacterial species can take up exogenous DNA by a process known as *transformation*.[†] Most transformable strains do not discriminate between uptake of DNA from a similar species and DNA from a completely different organism. Thus it should be relatively easy to introduce foreign DNA into bacteria. Probably the first recorded experiment of this kind is that of Abel & Trautner (1964). They reported that competent *Bacillus subtilis* could be transformed successfully with poxvirus DNA to yield infectious virions. However, current knowledge of poxvirus multiplication suggests that this result was an artefact.

Numerous groups of workers have reported the uptake of exogenous DNA by plant and animal cells and most of these experiments follow a

---

The sudden change of an animal cell possessing normal growth properties into one with many of the growth properties of the cancer cell is called *cell transformation*. Cell transformation is mentioned in chapter 8 and should not be confused with bacterial transformation which is described here.

similar pattern. The plant or animal cell is supplied with radioactive bacterial or viral DNA of a buoyant density different from that of the host. In general, the persistence of DNA of donor buoyant density over a period of time in host tissues has been taken as evidence for the continued presence of donor DNA, at least partially intact, within the plant or animal cell. The appearance of radioactivity at the buoyant density of the host DNA is sometimes observed. This could represent integration of small amounts of donor DNA into the host chromosome but more likely represents donor DNA which has been degraded and whose breakdown products have been reincorporated.

The majority of experiments involving DNA uptake by eukaryotes has emanated from Ledoux's laboratory at Moll (Ledoux & Huart 1968, Ledoux *et al.* 1971). Their early experiments involved barley grains which were dehusked and surface sterilized. Each seed was then sectioned 1 mm from the end distal to the embryo and immersed in radioactive DNA from *Micrococcus lysodeikticus*. After 72 h radioactive DNA could be extracted and this had a buoyant density of 1.712 g/cm³ compared with 1.702 g/cm³ for barley DNA and 1.731 g/cm³ for *M. lysodeikticus* DNA. Following sonication, DNA species with the densities of barley and micrococcal DNA were observed suggesting that this hybrid DNA consisted of covalently linked donor and recipient DNA. In similar experiments with *Arabidopsis thaliana* (a small weed) seedlings as host tissue, treatment of the F1 progeny, which had DNA of intermediate density, with more *M. lysodeikticus* DNA resulted in a new intermediate peak of greater buoyant density. This could be repeated over several generations producing peaks of greater density

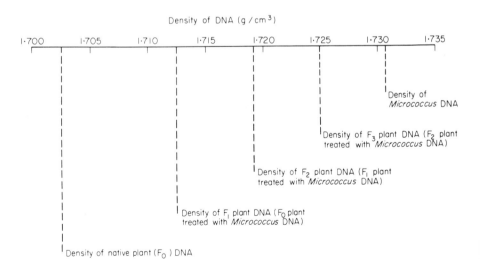

Fig. 1.1 Density of DNA from 'hybrids' of *Arabidopsis thaliana* and *Micrococcus lysodeikticus*. See text for details.

each time (Fig. 1.1). Ultrasonication again led to the production of DNA of host and donor buoyant densities.

There have been many attempts to repeat the experiments of Ledoux *et al.* but most have met with no success. Kleinhofs *et al.* (1975), for example, failed to observe such intermediate peaks when using axenic plants. However, when precautions against bacterial contamination failed, prominent intermediate peaks were observed and these were ascribed to bacteria growing on the roots. It would thus appear that foreign DNA is not integrated into the plant cell genome. The biggest problem with experiments like those of Ledoux and his colleagues is the determination of the fate of the exogenous DNA. It is apparent that density gradient centrifugation does not give unequivocal results. Much more sensitive techniques are available now (e.g. the 'Southern Blot' technique, page 7) and their development has greatly facilitated progress.

Transgenosis

Transgenosis is a term introduced by Doy *et al.* (1973) to describe the artificial transfer of genetic information from bacterial cells to eukaryotic cells by means of transducing phages. Four groups of workers have reported such experiments. Merril *et al.* (1971) took human fibroblasts from a patient with galactosaemia due to lack of galactose-1-phosphate uridyl transferase. The cells were infected with either λ *gal* T$^+$ or λ*gal* T$^-$ (where T specifies the transferase). Infected cells were assayed for phage-specific RNA and galactose-1-phosphate uridyl transferase. By four to five days after infection with phage as much as 0.2% of the total labelled RNA in the cells hybridized with λ DNA compared with less than 0.005% of the RNA from uninfected cells. Horst *et al.* (1975) used as recipient cells cultured skin fibroblasts from a patient with generalized gangliosidosis and characterized by a severe deficiency of β-galactosidase. The deficient human cells were incubated with the phage λ *plac or* λ *plac* DNA. The expression of the phage genome in the deficient fibroblasts could be demonstrated by detection of higher β-galactosidase activity after incubation with phage λ *plac* in 3 out of 19 experiments, and in 4 out of 16 experiments after treatment with λ *plac* DNA. λ *plac* DNA induced much higher enzyme activities than phage particles. The β-galactosidase activity in the infected fibroblasts was indistinguishable immunochemically and physicochemically from *E. coli* β-galactosidase. Doy *et al.* (1973) used ϕ80 *lac*$^+$ and λ *gal*$^+$ bacteriophage to treat haploid callus cultures of *Lycopersicon esculentum* (tomato) and *Arabidopsis thaliana*. These cultures grow on a defined medium containing glucose or sucrose but die when lactose or galactose is the sole carbon source. Treatment with the appropriate phage resulted in cultures which were able to grow on lactose or galactose, albeit more slowly than comparable calluses grown on glucose. The ability of these cultures to survive persisted over many subculturings and an immunological test confirmed the presence of the bacterial enzyme in the treated plant cells but not in the controls. Conceptually similar experiments to those of Doy *et al.* were performed at the same time by Johnson *et al.* (1973) with λ *lac* and cell suspension cultures of *Acer pseudoplatanus* (sycamore). After treatment with phage the cells were able to grow slowly on lactose whereas in the absence of bacteriophage or with λ⁺ the cells stopped growing and usually died. They were, however, unable to detect the bacterial enzyme either by assay or by electrophoresis.

Interesting as these experiments may be, considerably more evidence is needed to prove that *transgenosis* is a genuine phenomenon. There may be trivial reasons for the observed effects. Even so, transgenosis is purely of historical interest because it does not have the potential for large scale genetic manipulation afforded by other systems (see Chapters 3 and 4). The reason for this is set out below.

The Basic Problem

Although many people have attempted to transform pro- and eukaryotic cells with foreign DNA, transgenosis apart, their experiments have met with little success. Assuming that the exogenous DNA is taken up by the cells there are two basic reasons for the observed failures. Firstly, where detection of uptake is dependent on gene expression then failure could be due to lack of accurate transcription or translation. Secondly, and more importantly, the exogenous DNA may not be maintained in the transformed cells. If the exogenous DNA is integrated into the host genome then there is no problem. However, there are only two well-documented examples of this: the integration of plasmid DNA into the yeast genome (Hinnen *et al.* 1978, Struhl *et al.* 1979, see pp. 45-6) and the co-transformation of mouse cells with plasmid and phage DNA (Wigler *et al.* 1979, see page 100). The exact mechanism whereby this integration occurs is not clear. If the exogenous DNA fails to be integrated then it will probably be lost during subsequent multiplication of the host cells. The reason for this is simple. In order to be replicated DNA molecules must contain an *origin of replication* and in bacteria and viruses there is usually only one per genome. Such molecules are called *replicons*. Fragments of DNA are not replicons and in the absence of replication will be diluted out of their host cells. It should be noted that even if a DNA molecule contains an origin of replication this may not function in a foreign host cell.

The Basic Techniques

If fragments of DNA are not replicated then the obvious solution is to attach them to a suitable replicon. Such replicons are known as *vectors* or *cloning vehicles*. Small plasmids and bacteriophages are the most suitable vectors for they are replicons in their own right, their maintenance does not necessarily require integration into the host genome and their DNA can be isolated readily in an intact form. The different plasmids and phages which are used as vectors are described in detail in Chapters 3 and 4. Suffice it to say at this point that initially plasmids and phages suitable as vectors were only found in *Escherichia coli.*

Composite molecules in which foreign DNA has been inserted into a vector molecule are sometimes called DNA *chimaeras* because of their analogy with the Chimaera of mythology—a creature with the head of a lion, body of a goat and the tail of a serpent. The construction of such composite or *artificial recombinant* molecules has also been termed *genetic engineering* or *gene manipulation* because of the potential for creating novel genetic combinations by biochemical means. The process has also been termed *molecular cloning* or *gene cloning* because a line of genetically identical organisms, all of which contain the composite molecule, can be propagated and grown in bulk hence *amplifying* the composite molecule and any gene product whose synthesis it directs.

Although conceptually very simple, the insertion of a piece of foreign DNA into a vector demands that certain techniques be available. These are:

(1) mechanisms for cutting and joining DNA molecules from different sources,
(2) a method for monitoring the cutting and joining reactions, and
(3) a means of transforming *E. coli,* since the first vectors used functioned as replicons in this organism.

It is interesting to note that all three techniques were developed about the same time and quickly led to the first cloning experiments which were reported in 1972 (Jackson *et al.* 1972, Lobban & Kaiser 1973). The methods for cutting and joining DNA molecules are now so sophisticated that they warrant a chapter of their own (see Chapter 2). Further details on the transformation of *E. coli,* and the use of gel electrophoresis for monitoring the cutting and joining of DNA molecules are given in the next section.

Agarose Gel Electrophoresis
The progress of first experiments on the cutting and joining of DNA molecules was monitored by velocity sedimentation in sucrose gradients. However, velocity sedimentation through sucrose gradients has two disadvantages. Firstly, the DNA molecules have to be labelled and their position can only be detected by fractionating the gradient and measuring the radioactivity in each fraction. Secondly, DNA molecules of similar size are not resolved. Both these problems were overcome with the introduction of agarose gel electrophoresis.

As early as 1966, Thorne (1966, 1967) had demonstrated that agarose gel electrophoresis could be used to separate the different molecular configurations of polyoma viral DNA, e.g. covalently closed circular molecules,

nicked circles and linear molecules. However, a few years elapsed before
Aaij & Borst (1972) showed that electrophoresis in agarose gels could be
used to separate not only molecules of the same mol. wt. but different
configuration, but also molecules of different mol. wt. (Fig. 1.2). They
were also able to show that the migration rates of the molecules were
inversely proportional to the logarithms of their molecular weights thus
permitting accurate sizing of DNA molecules. Another advantage of
agarose gel electrophoresis is that the migration of DNA can readily be
detected without recourse to radio-labelling. The bands of DNA in the
gel are stained with the intercalating dye ethidium bromide and as little as
0.05 μg of DNA can be detected by direct examination of the gels in ultraviolet light.

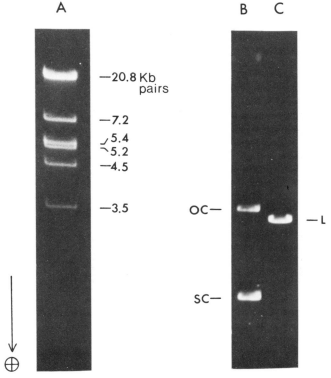

Fig. 1.2 Electrophoresis of DNA in agarose gels. The direction of migration is indicated by
the arrow. DNA bands have been visualized by soaking the gel in a solution of ethidium
bromide (which complexes with DNA by intercalating between stacked base pairs) and
photographing the orange fluorescence which results upon ultraviolet irradiation. (A) Phage
λ DNA restricted with *Eco* RI and then electrophoresed in a 1% agarose gel. The λ restriction
map is given in Fig. 4.4. (B) Open circular (OC) and super-coiled (SC) forms of a plasmid
of 6.4 Kb pairs. Note that the compact super-coils migrate considerably faster than open
circles. (C) Linear plasmid (L) DNA produced by treatment of the preparation shown in
lane B with *Eco* RI for which there is a single target site. Under the conditions of electrophoresis employed here, the linear form migrates just ahead of the open-circular form.
    The electrophoresis in lanes B and C was performed in a 0.7% agarose gel.

Readers wishing to know more about the factors affecting the electrophoretic mobility in agarose gels of the different conformational isomers of DNA should consult the paper of Johnson & Grossman (1977).

Frequently it is necessary to know what sequences in a DNA fragment are transcribed into RNA and, clearly, it would be helpful to have a method of detecting fragments in an agarose gel that are complementary to a given RNA. This can be done by slicing the gel, eluting the DNA, and hybridizing to DNA or RNA either in solution, or after binding the DNA to filters. This method, which is time consuming and inevitably leads to some loss in the resolving power of gel electrophoresis, has now been replaced by a neat method described by Southern (1975). This method, often referred to as *Southern blotting* is shown in Fig. 1.3. DNA in the gel is denatured by alkali treatment and the gel is then laid on top of buffer-saturated filter

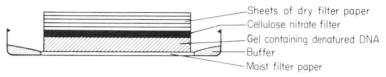

Fig. 1.3   The 'Southern blot' technique. See text for details.

paper. The top surface of the gel is covered with a cellulose nitrate filter and overlaid with dry filter paper. Buffer passes through the gel drawn by the dry filter paper and carries the DNA to the cellulose nitrate for which it has a high affinity. The DNA fragments bound to the cellulose nitrate can then be hybridized to radioactive DNA or RNA and hybrids detected by autoradiography.

Transformation of *E. coli*

Early attempts to achieve transformation of *E. coli* were unsuccessful and it was generally believed that *E. coli* was refractory to transformation. However, Mandel & Higa (1970) found that treatment with $CaCl_2$ allowed *E. coli* cells to take up DNA from bacteriophage λ. A few years later Cohen *et al.* (1972) showed that $CaCl_2$-treated *E. coli* cells are also effective recipients for plasmid DNA. The $CaCl_2$ probably causes changes in the structure of the cell wall that are necessary for uptake of DNA. Whereas almost any strain of *E. coli* can be transformed with plasmid DNA, albeit with varying efficiency, only *rec*BC⁻ mutants can be transformed with linear bacterial DNA (Cosley & Oishi 1973). RecBC⁻ mutants lack a nuclease which would otherwise degrade the DNA before it was integrated. Whereas linear bacterial DNA completely fails to transform RecBC⁺ cells, linear λ DNA transfects[†] them with 30% efficiency compared to RecBC⁻ cells.

Transformation of a cell with DNA from a virus is sometimes referred to as *transfection*. This term is used to indicate that the DNA is infectious, i.e. can give rise to progeny virus particles.

Why is there such a difference between linear bacterial and λDNA? Presumably the answer lies in the ability of λ DNA to circularize following uptake—a strategy which prevents it from attack by the RecBC exonuclease (Benzinger *et al.* 1975).

   The efficiency of transformation of *E. coli* is not high. Although efficiencies of 10^7 transformants/μg vector DNA can be achieved this represents uptake of only 1 DNA molecule/10^3 molecules added. With such low transformation efficiencies some cloning experiments are not feasible and currently much effort is being devoted to improving the efficiency of the process. As will be seen from the next chapter, many bacteria contain restriction systems which can influence the efficiency of transformation. Although the complete function of these restriction systems is not known yet, one role they do play is the recognition and degradation of foreign DNA. For this reason it is usual to use a 'restrictionless' (r⁻) mutant of *E. coli* as transformation host.

DNA Sequencing

This chapter would not be complete without giving at least passing mention to the techniques of DNA sequencing. Although the availability of such techniques is not *essential* to the success of a cloning experiment they do provide much useful information about the product formed. The principles behind these techniques are too complex to be discussed here but the interested reader is recommended to read the review article by Air (1979).

Chapter 2. Cutting and Joining
DNA Molecules

CUTTING DNA MOLECULES

It is worth recalling that prior to 1970 there was simply no method available for cutting a duplex DNA molecule into discrete fragments. DNA biochemistry was circumscribed by this impasse. It became apparent that the related phenomena of host-controlled restriction and modification might lead towards a solution to the problem when it was discovered that restriction involves specific endonucleases. The favourite organism of molecular biologists, *E. coli* K12, was the first to be studied in this regard, but turned out to be an unfortunate choice. Its endonuclease is perverse in the complexity of its behaviour. The breakthrough in 1970 came with the discovery in *Haemophilus influenzae* of an enzyme that behaves more simply. Present-day DNA technology is totally dependent upon our ability to cut DNA molecules at specific sites with restriction endonucleases. An account of host-controlled restriction and modification therefore forms the first part of this chapter.

Host-controlled Restriction and Modification

Host-controlled restriction and modification are most readily observed when bacteriophages are transferred from one bacterial host strain to another. If a stock preparation of phage λ, for example, is made by growth upon *E. coli* strain C and this stock is then titred upon *E. coli* C and *E. coli* K, the titres observed on these two strains will differ by several orders of magnitude, the titre on *E. coli* K being the lower. The phage are said to be *restricted* by the second host strain (*E. coli* K). When those phage that do result from the infection of *E. coli* K are now replated on *E. coli* K they are no longer restricted; but if they are first cycled through *E. coli* C they are once again restricted when plated upon *E. coli* K (Fig. 2.1). Thus the efficiency with which phage plates upon a particular host strain depends upon the strain on which it was last propagated. This non-heritable change conferred upon the phage by the second host strain (*E. coli* K) that allows it to be replated on that strain without further restriction is called modification.

The restricted phages adsorb to restrictive hosts and inject their DNA normally. When the phage are labelled with ^{32}P it is apparent that their DNA is degraded soon after injection (Dussoix & Arber 1962) and the

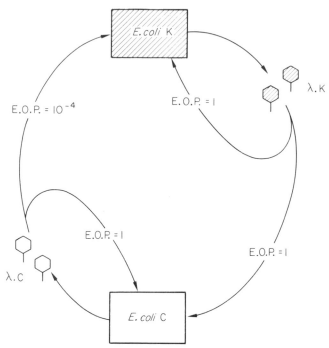

Fig. 2.1 Host-controlled restriction and modification of phage λ in *E. coli* strain K, analysed by efficiency of plating (E.O.P.). Phage propagated by growth on strains K or C (i.e. λ.K or λ.C) have E.O.P.s on the two strains as indicated by arrows. *E. coli* C has no known restriction and modification system.

endonuclease that is primarily responsible for this degradation is called a *restriction endonuclease* or restriction enzyme. The restrictive host must of course protect its own DNA from the potentially lethal effects of the restriction endonuclease and so its DNA must be appropriately modified. Modification involves methylation of certain bases at a very limited number of sequences within DNA which constitute the recognition sequences for the restriction endonuclease. This explains why phage that survive one cycle of growth upon the restrictive host can subsequently reinfect that host efficiently; their DNA has been replicated in the presence of the modifying methylase and so it, like the host DNA, becomes methylated and protected from the restriction system.

Although phage infection has been chosen as our example to illustrate restriction and modification, these processes can occur whenever DNA is transferred from one bacterial strain to another. Conjugation, transduction, transformation and transfection are all subject to the constraint of host-controlled restriction. The genes that specify host-controlled restriction and modification systems may reside upon the host chromosome itself or may be located on a plasmid or prophage such as P1.

The restriction endonuclease of *E. coli* K was the first to be isolated and studied in detail. Meselson & Yuan (1968) achieved this by devising an ingenious assay in which a fractionated cell extract was incubated with a mixture of unmodified and modified phage λ DNAs which were differentially radiolabelled—one with ^{3}H, the other with ^{32}P—so that they could be distinguished. After incubation, the DNA mixture was analysed by sedimentation through a sucrose gradient where the appearance of degraded unmodified DNA in the presence of undegraded modified DNA indicated the activity of restriction endonuclease.

The enzyme from *E. coli* K, and the similar one from *E. coli* B, were found to have unusual properties. In addition to magnesium ions, they require the cofactors ATP and S-adenosyl-methionine, and DNA degradation *in vitro* is accompanied by hydrolysis of the ATP in amounts greatly exceeding the stoichiometry of DNA breakage (Bickle *et al.* 1978). In addition, the enzymes are now known to interact with an unmodified *recognition* sequence in duplex DNA and then surprisingly, to track along the DNA molecule. The enzyme from *E. coli* B is known to track to one side only of the recognition sequence, which is asymmetric[†]. After travelling for a distance corresponding to between 1000 and 5000 nucleotides it cleaves one strand only of the DNA at an apparently random site, and makes a gap about 75 nucleotides in length by releasing acid-soluble oligonucleotides. There is no evidence that the enzyme is truly catalytic, and having acted once in this way, a second enzyme molecule is required to complete the double-strand break (Rosamond *et al.* 1979). Enzymes with these properties are now known as type I restriction endonucleases. Their biochemistry still presents many puzzles. For instance, the precise role of S-adenosyl-methionine remains unclear.

While these bizarre properties of type I restriction enzymes were being unravelled, a restriction endonuclease from *Haemophilus influenzae* Rd was discovered (Kelly & Smith 1970, Smith & Wilcox 1970) that was to become the prototype of a large number of restriction endonucleases— now known as type II enzymes—that have none of the unusual properties displayed by type I enzymes and which are fundamentally important in the manipulation of DNA. The type II enzymes recognize a particular target sequence in a duplex DNA molecule and break the polynucleotide chains within that sequence to give rise to discrete DNA fragments of defined length and sequence. In fact, the activity of these enzymes is often assayed and studied by gel electrophoresis of the DNA fragments which they generate (see Fig. 1.2). As expected, digests of small plasmid or viral DNAs give characteristic simple DNA band patterns.

[†] The recognition sequence of the restriction endonuclease of *E. coli* B is known:

$$5' \ TGA \ (N)_8 TGCT \ 3'$$
$$3' \ ACT \ (N)_8 ACGA \ 5'$$

Very many type II restriction endonucleases have now been isolated from a wide variety of bacteria. In a recent review, Roberts (1978) lists 168 enzymes that have been at least partially characterized, and the number continues to grow as more bacterial genera are surveyed for their presence. It is worth noting that many so-called restriction endonucleases have not formally been shown to correspond with any genetically identified restriction and modification system of the bacteria from which they have been prepared: it is usually assumed that a site-specific endonuclease which is inactive upon host DNA and active upon exogenous DNA is, in fact, a restriction endonuclease.

Nomenclature

The discovery of a large number of restriction enzymes called for a uniform nomenclature. A system based upon the proposals of Smith & Nathans (1973) has been followed for the most part. The proposals were as follows:

(1) The species name of the host organism is identified by the first letter of the genus name and the first two letters of the specific epithet to form a three-letter abbreviation in italics. For example, *Escherichia coli = Eco* and *Haemophilus influenzae = Hin.*

(2) Strain or type identification is written as a subscript, e.g. Eco_K. In cases where the restriction and modification system is genetically specified by a virus or plasmid, the abbreviated species name of the host is given and the extrachromosomal element is identified by a subscript, e.g. Eco_{PI}, Eco_{RI}.

(3) When a particular host strain has several different restriction and modification systems, these are identified by Roman numerals, thus the systems from *H. influenzae* strain Rd would be $Hin_d I$, $Hin_d II$, $Hin_d III$, etc.

(4) All restriction enzymes have the general name endonuclease R, but, in addition, carry the system name, e.g. endonuclease R. $Hin_d III$. Similarly, modification enzymes are named methylase M followed by the system name. The modification enzyme from *H. influenzae* Rd corresponding to endonuclease R. $Hin_d III$ is designated methylase M. $Hin_d III$.

In practice this system of nomenclature has been simplified further.

(1) Subscripts are typographically inconvenient: the whole abbreviation is now usually written on the line.

(2) Where the context makes it clear that restriction enzymes only are involved, the designation endonuclease R. is omitted. This is the system used in Table 2.1, which lists some of the more commonly used restriction endonucleases.

Type II restriction endonucleases recognize and break DNA within particular sequences of tetra- , penta- , hexa- or heptanucleotides which have an axis of rotational symmetry. For example, *Eco* RI cuts at the

Table 2.1   Taret sites of some restriction endonucleases.

Anabaena variabilis	*Ava* I	C↓(T)CG(G)G (C/A above)	
Bacillus amyloliquefaciens H	*Bam* HI	G↓GATCC	
Bacillus globigii	*Bgl* II	A↓GATCT	
Escherichia coli RY13	*Eco* RI	G↓A*ATTC	1,4
Escherichia coli R245	*Eco* RII	↓CC(T)GG (A above)	2
Haemophilus aegyptius	*Hae* III	GG↓C*C	
Haemophilus gallinarum	*Hga* I	GACGC	3
Haemophilus haemolyticus	*Hha* I	GC*G↓C	
Haemophilus influenzae Rd	*Hind* II	GT(T)↓(G)AC (C/A* above)	
	Hind III	A*↓AGCTT	
Haemophilus parainfluenzae	*Hpa* I	GTT↓AAC	
	Hpa II	C↓C*GG	
Klebsiella pneumoniae	*Kpn* I	GGTAC↓C	
Moraxella bovis	*Mbo* I	↓GATC	
Providencia stuartii	*Pst* I	CTGCA↓G	
Serratia marcescens	*Sma* I	CCC↓GGG	
Streptomyces stanford	*Sst* I	GAGCT↓C	
Xanthomonas malvacearum	*Xma* I	C↓CCGGG	

Source: Roberts (1978). Recognition sequences are written from $5' \rightarrow 3'$ only one strand being given, and the point of cleavage is indicated by an arrow. Bases written in parentheses signify that either base may occupy that position. Where known, the base modified by the corresponding specific methylase is indicated by an asterisk. $\overset{*}{A}$ is N^6-methyladenine, $\overset{*}{C}$ is 5-methylcytosine.

Notes

1,2. The names of these two enzymes are anomalous. The genes specifying the enzymes are borne on two Resistance Transfer Factors which have been classified separately. Hence RI and RII.

3. *Hga*I is a Type III restriction endonuclease, cleaving as indicated:

    5′   GACGCNNNNN↓

    3′   CTGCGNNNNN NNNNN↓

4. Under certain conditions (low ionic strength, alkaline pH or 50% glycerol) the *Eco* RI specificity is reduced so that only the internal tetranucleotide sequence of the canonical hexanucleotide is necessary for recognition and cleavage. This is so-called *Eco* RI* (RI-star) activity. It is inhibited by parachloromercuribenzoate, whereas *Eco* RI activity is insensitive (Tikchonenko *et al.* 1978).

positions indicated by arrows in the sequence

$$\begin{array}{c} \text{axis of symmetry} \\ 5' - G\overset{\downarrow}{A}\overset{*}{A} \mid T\,T\,C - \\ 3' - C\,T\,T \mid \underset{*}{A}\,A\underset{\uparrow}{G} - \end{array}$$

giving rise to termini bearing 5'-phosphate and 3'-hydroxyl groups. Such sequences are sometimes said to be *palindromic* by analogy with words that read alike backwards and forwards. (However, this term has also been applied to sequences such as

$$\begin{array}{c} 5' - A\,G\,C\,C\,G\,A - \\ 3' - T\,C\,G\,G\,C\,T - \end{array}$$

which are palindromic *within one strand,* yet do not have an axis of rotational symmetry.) If the sequence is modified by methylation so that 6-methyladenine residues are found at *one or both* of the positions indicated by asterisks then the sequence is resistant to endonuclease R. *Eco* RI. The resistance of the half-methylated site protects the bacterial host's own duplex DNA from attack immediately after semi-conservative replication of the fully-methylated site until the modification methylase can once again restore the daughter duplexes to the fully-methylated state.

We can see that *Eco* RI makes single-strand breaks four nucleotide pairs apart in the opposite strands of its target sequence, and so generates fragments with protruding 5'-termini. These DNA fragments can associate by hydrogen bonding between overlapping 5'-termini, or the fragments can circularize by intramolecular reaction, and for this reason the fragments are said to have *sticky* or *cohesive* ends (Fig. 2.2). In principle, DNA fragments from diverse sources can be joined by means of the cohesive ends, and it is possible, as we shall see later, to seal the remaining nicks in the two strands to form an intact *artificially recombinant* duplex DNA molecule.

It is clear from Table 2.1 that not all type II enzymes have target sites like *Eco* RI. Some enzymes (e.g. *Pst* I) produce fragments bearing 3'-cohesive ends. Others (e.g. *Hae* III) make even cuts giving rise to flush- or blunt-ended fragments with no cohesive end at all. Some enzymes recognize tetranucleotide sequences, others recognize longer sequences. We would expect any particular tetranucleotide target to occur about once every 4^4 (i.e. 256) nucleotide pairs in a long random DNA sequence, assuming all bases are equally frequent. Any particular hexanucleotide target would be expected to occur once in every 4^6 (i.e. 4096) nucleotide pairs. Some enzymes (e.g. *Mbo* I) recognize a tetranucleotide sequence that is included within the hexanucleotide sequence recognized by a different enzyme (e.g. *Bam* HI). *Hind* II, the first type II enzyme to be discovered, is an example of an enzyme recognizing a sequence with some ambiguity; in this case all three sequences corresponding to the structure given in Table 2.1 are substrates.

INTERMOLECULAR ASSOCIATION   INTRAMOLECULAR ASSOCIATION

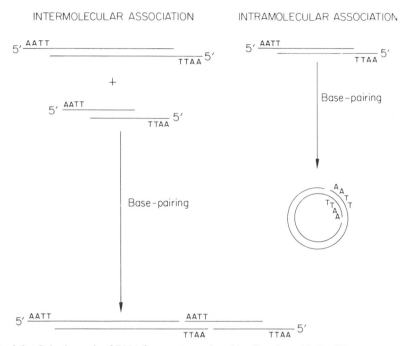

Fig. 2.2   Cohesive ends of DNA fragments produced by digestion with *Eco* RI.

There are also several known examples of enzymes from different sources
which recognize the same target. They are *isoschizomers*. Some pairs of
isoschizomers cut their target at different places (e.g. *Sma* I, *Xma* I).
    Recently, a third class of restriction endonuclease has been identified.
Type III enzymes make breaks in the two strands at *measured distances*
to one side of their target sequence (e.g. *Hga* I). This variety of properties
exhibited by restriction endonucleases provides scope for the ingenious and
resourceful gene manipulator.
    What is the function of restriction endonucleases *in vivo*? Clearly host-
controlled restriction acts as a mechanism by which bacteria distinguish
self from non-self. It is analogous to an immunity system. Restriction is
moderately effective in preventing infection by some bacteriophages. It
may be for this reason that the T-even phages (T2, T4 and T6) have evolved
with glucosylated hydroxymethylcytosine residues replacing cytosine in
their DNA, so rendering it resistant to many restriction endonucleases.
The restriction and glucosylation modification of T-even phage DNA is
beyond the scope of this book. For a detailed discussion the reader is
referred to Kornberg (1974). However, it is worth noting that a mutant
strain of T4 is available which does have cytosine residues in its DNA and is
therefore amenable to conventional restriction methodology (Velten *et al.*
1976). As an alternative to the unusual DNA structure of the T-even phages,

other mechanisms appear to have evolved in T3 and T7 for overcoming restriction *in vivo* (Spoerel *et al.* 1979). In spite of this evidence we may be mistaken in concluding that immunity to phage infection is the sole or main function of restriction endonucleases in nature; loss or alteration of phage receptors might be a more economical way of achieving immunity. For the present we can only speculate.

Mechanical Shearing of DNA

In addition to digesting DNA with restriction endonucleases to produce discrete fragments, there are a variety of treatments which result in non-specific breakage. Non-specific endonucleases and chemical degradation can be used but the only method that has been much applied to gene manipulation involves mechanical shearing.

The long, thin threads which constitute duplex DNA molecules are sufficiently rigid to be very easily broken by shear forces in solution. Intense sonication with ultrasound can reduce the length to about 300 nucleotide pairs. More controlled shearing can be achieved by high-speed stirring in a blender. Typically, high mol. wt. DNA is sheared to a population of molecules with a mean size of about 8 Kb pairs by stirring at 1500 rev/min for 30 min (Wensink *et al.* 1974). Breakage occurs essentially at random with respect to DNA sequence producing termini consisting of short single-stranded regions which may have to be taken into account in subsequent joining procedures.

JOINING DNA MOLECULES

Having described the methods available for cutting DNA molecules we must consider the ways in which DNA fragments can be joined to create artificially recombinant molecules. There are currently three methods for joining DNA fragments *in vitro*. The first of these capitalizes on the ability of DNA ligase to join covalently the annealed cohesive ends produced by certain restriction enzymes. The second depends upon the ability of DNA ligase from phage T4-infected *E. coli* to catalyse the formation of phospho-diester bonds between blunt-ended fragments. The third utilizes the enzyme terminal deoxynucleotidyl-transferase to synthesize homopolymeric 3′-single-stranded tails at the ends of fragments. We can now look at these three methods a little more deeply.

DNA Ligase

E. coli and phage T4 produce an enzyme, DNA ligase, which seals single-stranded nicks between adjacent nucleotides in a duplex DNA chain (Olivera *et al.* 1968, Gumport & Lehman 1971). Although the reactions catalysed by the enzymes of *E. coli* and T4-infected *E. coli* are very similar, they differ in their cofactor requirements. The T4 enzyme requires ATP,

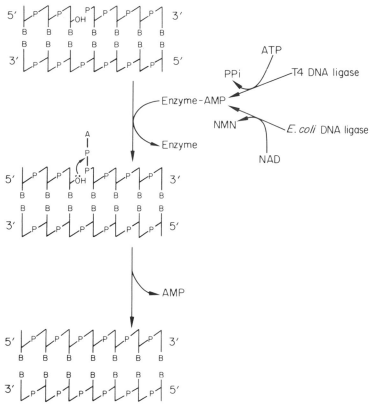

Fig. 2.3 Action of DNA ligase. An enzyme-AMP complex binds to a nick bearing 3′-OH and 5′-P groups. The AMP reacts with the phosphate group. Attack by the 3′-OH group on this moiety generates a new phosphodiester bond which seals the nick.

whilst the *E. coli* enzyme requires NAD. In each case the cofactor is split and forms an enzyme-AMP complex. The complex binds to the nick, which must expose a 5′-phosphate and 3′-OH group, and makes a covalent bond in the phosphodiester chain as shown in Fig. 2.3.

When termini created by a restriction endonuclease which creates cohesive ends associate, the joint has nicks a few base pairs apart in opposite strands. DNA ligase can then repair these nicks to form an intact duplex. This reaction, performed *in vitro* with purified DNA ligase, is fundamental to many gene manipulation procedures, such as that shown in Fig. 2.4.

The optimum temperature for ligation of nicked DNA is 37°C, but at this temperature the hydrogen-bonded joint between the sticky ends is unstable. *Eco* RI-generated termini associate through only four A.T base pairs and these are not sufficient to resist thermal disruption at such a high temperature. The optimum temperature for ligating the cohesive termini is therefore a compromise between the rate of enzyme action and association

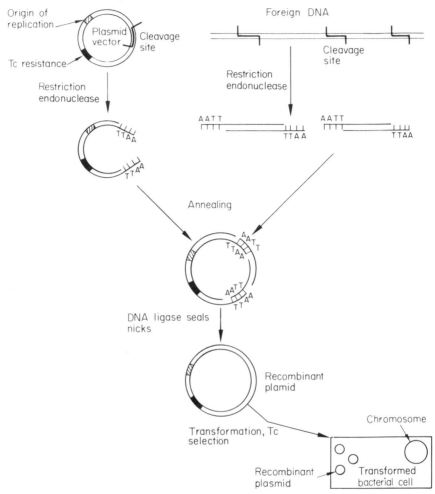

Fig. 2.4 Use of DNA ligase to create a covalent DNA recombinant joined through association of termini generated by *Eco* RI.

of the termini, and has been found by experiment to be about 15°C (Dugaiczyk *et al.* 1975).

The ligation reaction can be performed so as to favour the formation of recombinants. Firstly, the proportion of recombinants can be increased by performing the reaction at a high DNA concentration; in dilute solutions *circularization* of linear fragments is relatively favoured because of the reduced frequency of intermolecular reactions. Secondly, by treating linearized plasmid vector DNA with alkaline phosphatase to remove 5′-terminal phosphate groups, both recircularization and plasmid dimer formation are prevented (Fig. 2.5). In this case, circularization of the vector can occur only by insertion of un-phosphatased foreign DNA which

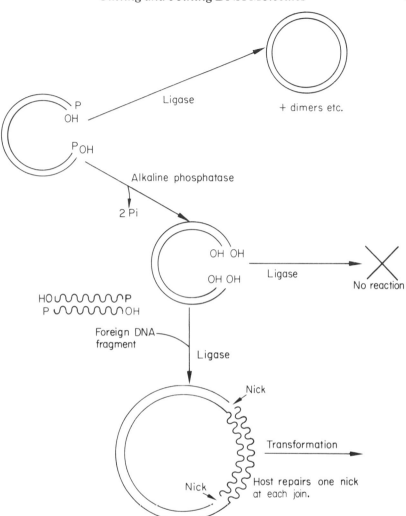

Fig. 2.5 Application of alkaline phosphatase treatment to prevent recircularization of vector plasmid without insertion of foreign DNA.

provides one 5′-terminal phosphate at each join. One nick at each join remains unligated, but after transformation of host bacteria cellular repair mechanisms reconstitute the intact duplex.

Joining DNA fragments with cohesive ends by DNA ligase is a relatively efficient process which has been used extensively to create artificial recombinants. A modification of this procedure depends upon the ability of T4 DNA ligase, but not *E. coli* DNA ligase, to join blunt-ended DNA molecules (Sgaramella 1972). This procedure is most usefully applied to joining blunt-ended fragments via *linker* molecules. For example, Scheller

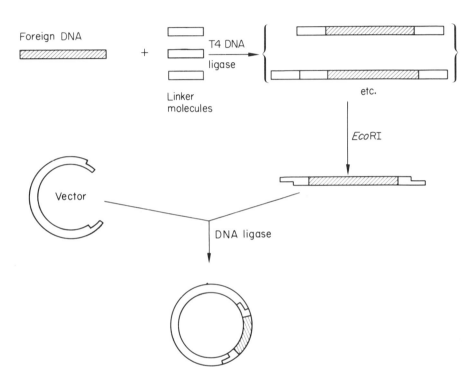

Fig. 2.6 A decameric linker molecule containing an *Eco* RI target site is joined by T4 DNA ligase to both ends of flush-ended foreign DNA. Cohesive ends are then generated by *Eco* RI. This DNA can then be incorporated into a vector that has been treated with the same restriction endonuclease.

et al. (1977), have synthesized self-complementary decameric oligonucleotides which contain sites for one or more restriction endonucleases. One such molecule is shown in Fig. 2.6. The molecule can be ligated to both ends of the foreign DNA to be cloned, and then treated with restriction endonuclease to produce a sticky-ended fragment which can be incorporated into a vector molecule that has been cut with the same restriction endonuclease. Insertion by means of the linker creates restriction enzyme target sites at each end of the foreign DNA, and so enables the foreign DNA to be excised and recovered after cloning and amplification in the host bacterium.

Homopolymer Tailing

A general method for joining DNA molecules makes use of the annealing of complementary homopolymer sequences. Thus, by adding oligo (dA) sequences to the 3'-ends of one population of DNA molecules, and oligo (dT) blocks to the 3'-ends of another population, the two types of molecule can anneal to form mixed dimeric circles (Fig. 2.7).

An enzyme purified from calf-thymus, terminal deoxynucleotidyl-transferase, provides the means by which the homopolymeric extensions can be synthesized. For if presented with a single deoxynucleotide tri-phosphate it will repeatedly add nucleotides to the 3'-OH termini of a population of DNA molecules (Chang & Bollum 1971). DNA with exposed 3'-OH groups, such as arise from pretreatment with phage λ exonuclease or restriction with an enzyme such as *Pst* I, is a very good substrate for the transferase. However, conditions have been found in which the enzyme will extend even the shielded 3'-OH of 5'-cohesive termini generated by *Eco* RI (Roychoudhury *et al.* 1976, Humphries *et al.* 1978).

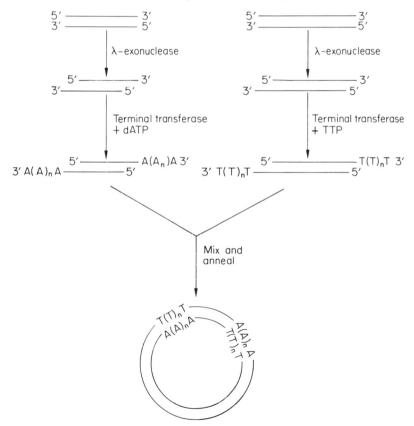

Fig. 2.7 Use of calf-thymus terminal deoxynucleotidyl transferase to add complementary homopolymer tails to two DNA molecules.

Chapter 3. Plasmids as Cloning Vehicles

Basic Properties of Plasmids

Plasmids are widely used as cloning vehicles but before discussing their use in this context it is appropriate to review some of their basic properties. Plasmids are replicons which are stably inherited in an extra-chromosomal state. It should be emphasized that extrachromosomal nucleic acid molecules are not necessarily plasmids, for the definition given above implies genetic homogeneity, constant monomeric unit size and the ability to replicate independently of the chromosome. Thus the heterogeneous circular DNA molecules which are found in *Bacillus megaterium* (Carlton & Helinski 1969) are not necessarily plasmids. The definition given above, however, does include the prophages of those temperate phages, e.g. P1, which are maintained in an extrachromosomal state, as opposed to those such as λ (see next chapter) which are maintained by integration into the host chromosome. Also included are the replicative forms of the filamentous coliphages which specify the continued production and release of phage particles without concomitant cell lysis.

Plasmids are widely distributed throughout the prokaryotes, vary in size from less than 1×10^6 daltons to greater than 200×10^6, and are generally dispensable. Some of the phenotypes which these plasmids confer on their host cells are listed in Table 3.1. Plasmids to which phenotypic traits have not yet been ascribed are called *cryptic* plasmids.

Table 3.1 Phenotypic traits exhibited by plasmid-carried genes.

Antibiotic resistance	Heavy-metal resistance
Antibiotic production	Bacteriocin production
Degradation of aromatic compounds	Induction of plant tumours
Haemolysin production	Hydrogen sulphide production
Sugar fermentation	Host-controlled restriction and modification
Enterotoxin production	

Plasmids can be categorized into one of the two major types—conjugative or non-conjugative—depending on whether or not they carry a set of genes, called the *tra* genes, that promotes bacterial conjugation. Plasmids can also be categorized on the basis of their being maintained as multiple copies per cell (*relaxed* plasmids) or as a limited number of copies per cell (*stringent* plasmids). The replication of stringent plasmids is of necessity coupled to chromosome replication, hence their low copy number. Generally, conjugative plasmids are of a relatively high mol. wt. and are present as 1-3 copies per chromosome whereas non-conjugative plasmids are of low mol. wt. and present as multiple copies per cell (Table 3.2). An exception is the conjugative plasmid R6K which has a mol. wt. of 25×10^6 daltons and is maintained as a relaxed plasmid.

Table 3.2 Properties of some conjugative and non-conjugative plasmids.

Plasmid	Size (Mdal.)	Conjugative	No. of plasmid copies/cell	Phenotype
Col E1	4.2	no	10-15	Colicin E1 production
RSF 1030	5.6	no	20-40	ampicillin resistance
clo DF13	6	no	10	cloacin production
R6K	25	yes	13-38	ampicillin and streptomycin resistance
F	62	yes	1-2	—
RI	65	yes	1-3	multiple drug resistance
R6	65	yes	1-3	multiple drug resistance
Ent P 307	65	yes	1-3	enterotoxin production

Plasmid *incompatibility* is the inability of two different plasmids to coexist in the same host cell in the absence of selection pressure. The term incompatibility can only be used when it is certain that entry of the second plasmid has taken place and that DNA restriction is not involved. Groups of plasmids which are mutually incompatible are considered to belong to the same incompatibility class. Currently, over 25 incompatibility groups have been defined among plasmids of *E. coli* and 7 for plasmids of *Staphylococcus aureus*. With one exception, incompatibility is of relatively little importance for gene manipulation. Plasmids belonging to incompatibility class P, e.g. RP4, are termed *promiscuous* for they are capable of promoting their own transfer to a wide range of Gram-negative bacteria and of being stably maintained in these diverse hosts. Such promiscuous plasmids thus offer the potential of readily transferring cloned DNA molecules into a wide range of genetic environments.

An extremely useful article explaining the terminology used in plasmid genetics is that of Novick *et al.* (1976). A much fuller discussion of the topics outlined above is provided by Falkow (1975).

The Purification of Plasmid DNA

An obvious prerequisite for cloning in plasmids is the purification of the plasmid DNA. Although a wide range of plasmid DNAs are now routinely purified the methods used are not without their problems. Undoubtedly the trickiest stage is the lysis of the host cells: both incomplete lysis and total dissolution of the cells result in greatly reduced recoveries of plasmid DNA. The ideal situation occurs when each cell is just sufficiently broken to permit the plasmid DNA to escape without too much contaminating chromosomal DNA. Provided the lysis is done gently most of the chromosomal DNA which is released will be of high mol. wt. and can be removed, along with cell debris, by high speed centrifugation to yield a *cleared lysate.* The production of satisfactory cleared lysates from bacteria other than *E. coli* and *B. subtilis,* particularly if large plasmids are to be isolated, is frequently a combination of skill, luck and patience.

Many methods are available for isolating pure plasmid DNA from cleared lysates but only two will be described here. The first of these is the 'classical' method and is due to Vinograd (Radloff *et al.* 1967). This method involves isopycnic centrifugation of cleared lysates in CsCl containing ethidium bromide (EtBr). EtBr binds by intercalating between the DNA base pairs and in so doing causes the DNA to unwind. A covalently closed circular (CCC) DNA molecule such as a plasmid has no free ends and can only unwind to a limited extent thus limiting the amount of EtBr bound. A linear DNA molecule, such as fragmented chromosomal DNA, has no such topological constraints and can therefore bind more of the EtBr molecules. Because the density of the DNA/EtBr complex decreases as more EtBr is bound, and because more EtBr can be bound to a linear molecule than a

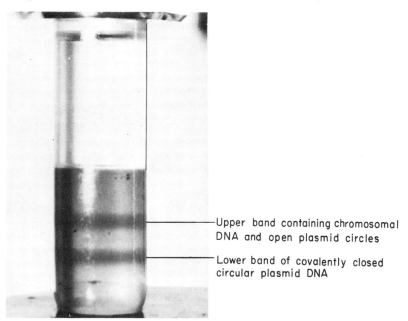

Upper band containing chromosomal DNA and open plasmid circles

Lower band of covalently closed circular plasmid DNA

Fig. 3.1   Purification of ColEI kan ᴿ plasmid DNA by isopycnic centrifugation in a CsCl-EtBr gradient. (Photo by courtesy of Dr. G. Birnie.)

covalent circle, the covalent circle has a higher density at saturating concentrations of EtBr. Thus covalent circles (i.e. plasmids) can be separated from linear chromosomal DNA (Fig. 3.1).

The above method suffers from a number of disadvantages: it is expensive in both centrifuge time and materials, has limited capacity, and complete removal of the ethidium bromide is both difficult and tedious. An alternative method which is both rapid and inexpensive is to chromatograph the cleared lysate on hydroxylapatite (Colman *et al.* 1978). Initially conditions are chosen to ensure that all double-stranded DNA is retained by the hydroxylapatite but contaminating RNA and protein are washed through. The DNA is then eluted from the column and consists almost entirely (> 99%) of plasmid DNA, chromosomal DNA being physically retained presumably because of its higher mol. wt. and extended configuration.

Desirable Properties of Plasmid Cloning Vehicles

An ideal cloning vehicle would have the following three properties:
(1) Low molecular weight;
(2) Ability to confer readily selectable phenotypic traits on host cells;
(3) Single sites for a large number of restriction endonucleases, preferably in genes with a readily scorable phenotype.

The advantages of a low mol. wt. are severalfold. Firstly, the plasmid is much easier to handle, i.e. it is more resistant to damage by shearing, and is readily isolated from host cells. Secondly, low mol. wt. plasmids are usually present as multiple copies (Table 3.2) and this not only facilitates their isolation but leads to gene dosage effects for all cloned genes. Finally, with a low mol. wt. there is less chance that the vector will have multiple substrate sites for any restriction endonuclease (see below).

After a piece of foreign DNA is inserted into a vector the resulting chimaeric molecules have to be transformed into a suitable recipient. Since the efficiency of transformation is so low it is essential that the chimaera have some readily scorable phenotype. Usually this results from some gene, e.g. antibiotic resistance, carried on the vector but could also be produced by a gene carried on the inserted DNA.

One of the first steps in cloning is to cut the vector DNA and the DNA to be inserted with the same endonuclease. If the vector has more than one site for the endonuclease then more than one fragment will be produced. When the two samples of cleaved DNA are subsequently mixed and ligated the resulting chimaeras will, in all probability, lack one of the vector fragments. It is advantageous if insertion of foreign DNA at endonuclease-sensitive sites inactivates a gene whose phenotype is readily scorable, for in this way it is possible to distinguish chimaeras from cleaved plasmid molecules which have self-annealed. Of course, readily detectable insertional inactivation is not essential if the vector and insert are to be joined by the homopolymer tailing method (see page 21) or if the insert confers a new phenotype on host cells.

Some examples will be presented which illustrate the points raised above but first we shall consider how some of the common plasmids rate as cloning vehicles.

Usefulness of 'Natural' Plasmids as Cloning Vehicles

The term 'natural' is used loosely in this context to describe plasmids which were not constructed *in vitro* for the sole purpose of cloning. Col E1 is a naturally occurring plasmid which specifies the production of a bacteriocin, colicin E1. By necessity this plasmid also carries a gene which confers on host cells immunity to colicin E1. RSF 2124 is a derivative of Col E1 which carries a transposon specifying ampicillin resistance. The exact origin of pSC101 is not clear but for the purposes of this discussion we shall consider it to be a 'natural' plasmid. Details of these plasmids are shown in Table 3.3.

Table 3.3   Properties of some 'natural' plasmids used for cloning DNA.

Plasmid	Size (Mdal.)	Single sites for endonucleases	Marker for selecting transformants	Insertional inactivation of
pSC101	5.8	*Eco* RI	tetracycline resistance	—
Col E1	4.2	*Eco* RI	immunity to colicin E1	colicin E1 production
RSF 2124	7.4	*Eco* RI	ampicillin resistance	colicin E1 production
		Bam HI	ampicillin resistance	colicin E1 production

To clone DNA in pSC101, the plasmid DNA and the DNA to be inserted are digested with *Eco* RI, mixed and treated with DNA ligase. The ligated molecules are then used to transform a suitable recipient to tetracycline-resistance. Unfortunately there is no easy genetical method of distinguishing chimaeras from reconstituted vector DNA unless the insert confers a new phenotype on the transformants. Two examples of the use of pSC101 for cloning DNA are presented in the next section. Cloning with Col E1 as the vector is a little simpler. Transformants are selected on the basis of immunity to colicin E1 and chimaeras recognized by their inability to produce colicin E1. Unfortunately screening for immunity to colicin E1 is not technically simple and plasmid RSF 2124 is more useful in this respect since transformants are selected by virtue of their ampicillin resistance.

Col E1 and plasmids derived from it (see later) have a distinct advantage over pSC101—they can be enriched with chloramphenicol. When chloramphenicol is added to a late log-phase culture of a Col E1-containing strain of *E. coli,* chromosome replication ceases because of the need for continued protein synthesis. However, the cessation of protein synthesis has no effect on Col E1 replication such that after 10-12 hours over 50% of the DNA in the cells is plasmid DNA (Hershfield *et al.* 1974). Since there may be 1000-3000 copies of the plasmid in each cell it is easy to see why chloramphenicol enrichment is a useful step in plasmid isolation.

Example of the Use of pSC101 for Cloning. 1. Expression of *Staphylococcus* Plasmid Genes in *E. coli*

For this experiment Chang & Cohen (1974) considered *Staph. aureus* plasmid pI258 (mol. wt. 20 × 10⁶) as being particularly appropriate for experiments involving interspecies genome construction since it carries several different genetic determinants that were potentially detectable in *E. coli.* Moreover, agarose gel electrophoresis indicated that this plasmid is cleaved by the *Eco* RI restriction endonuclease into four easily identifiable fragments. Molecular chimaeras containing DNA derived from both *Staphylococcus* and *E. coli* were constructed by ligation of a mixture of *Eco* RI-cleaved pSC101 and pI258 DNA and then were used to transform a restrictionless strain of *E. coli* (Fig. 3.2). *E. coli* transformants that expressed

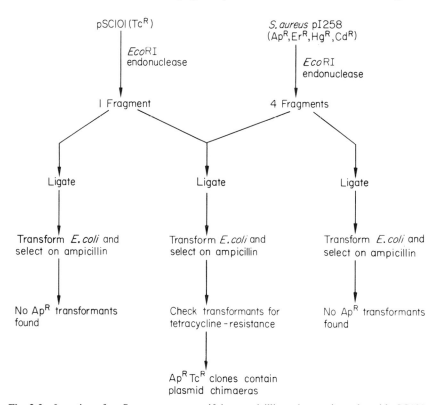

Fig. 3.2   Insertion of an *S. aureus* gene specifying ampicillin-resistance into plasmid pSC101.

the penicillin resistance determinant carried by the *Staphylococcus* plasmid were selected and checked for tetracycline resistance.

    Caesium chloride gradient analysis of one ampicillin-resistant, tetracycline-resistant chimaera showed that its buoyant density was intermediate to the buoyant densities of the parental plasmids. In addition, treatment of this chimaera with *Eco* RI produced two fragments, one the size of *Eco* RI cleaved pSC101 and the other the size of one of the *Eco* RI fragments of pI258.

Example of the Use of pSC101 for Cloning. 2. Cloning of *Xenopus* DNA in *E. coli*

This experiment by Morrow *et al.* (1974) involved the *in vitro* construction of plasmid chimaeras composed of both prokaryotic and eukaryotic DNA, and the recovery of recombinant DNA molecules from transformed *E. coli* in the absence of selection for genetic determinants carried by the eukaryotic DNA. The amplified ribosomal DNA from *Xenopus laevis*

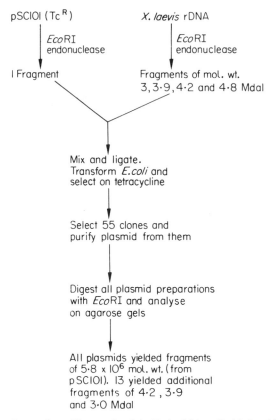

Fig. 3.3 Cloning of genes from *Xenopus laevis* in *Escherichia coli* with the aid of pSC101.

oocytes (see page 60) was used as the source of eukaryotic DNA for these experiments since this DNA can be purified readily and has been well characterized. In addition, the repeat unit of *X. laevis* rDNA is susceptible to cleavage by *Eco* RI resulting in the production of discrete fragments that can be linked to the pSC101 vector.

In this experiment (Fig. 3.3) a mixture of *Eco* RI-cleaved pSC101 DNA and *X. laevis* rDNA was ligated and was used to transform *E. coli* to tetracycline-resistance. Fifty five separate transformants were selected and their plasmid DNA extracted and analysed. All 55 plasmids gave a fragment of mol. wt. 5.8×10^6 on *Eco* RI digestion and 13 of them yielded additional fragments corresponding in size to *Eco* RI produced fragments of *X. laevis* rDNA. It was indeed fortuitous that such a high percentage (23.6%) of clones contained chimaeric molecules.

Construction and Characterization of New Cloning Vehicles

Although pSC101, Col E1 and RSF 2124 can be used to clone DNA they suffer from a number of disadvantages as outlined above. For this reason, considerable effort has been expended on constructing *in vitro* superior cloning vehicles. The properties of some of these artificial vectors are shown in Table 3.4.

Undoubtedly the most widely used of these artificial plasmid vectors is pBR322. Plasmid pBR322 contains the Ap^R and Tc^R genes derived from pRSF 2124 and pSC101 respectively combined with replication elements of pMB9, a Col E1-like plasmid. Details of the construction of pBR322, and its progenitor pBR313, are too complex to outline here, but can be

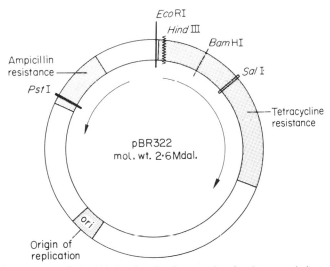

Fig. 3.4   The structure of pBR322 showing the cleavage sites for those restriction endonucleases which cut the DNA only once. The arrows inside the circle show the direction of transcription of Ap^R and Tc^R genes.

EcoRI

Met Ala Gly Cys Lys Asn Phe Phe Trp Lys Thr Phe Thr Ser Cys Stop Stop

5′ AATTCATGGCTGGTTGTAAGAACTTCTTTTGGAAGACTTTCACTTCGTGTTGATAG
    GTACCGACCAACATTCTTGAAGAAAACCTTCTGAAAGTGAAGCACAACTATCCTAG 5′

BamHI

Fig. 3.5 Sequence of the chemically synthesized somatostatin gene.

In the first part of the experiment three new plasmids were created from pBR322. The control region of the *lac* operon, comprising the *lac* promoter, catabolite gene activator-protein binding site, the operator, the ribosome binding site, and the first seven triplets of the β-galactosidase structural

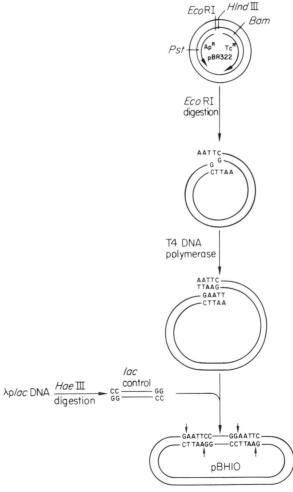

Fig. 3.6 The formation of pBH10 by insertion of the *lac* control region into pBR322. Note the generation of two *Eco* RI sites, one on either side of the *lac* control region.

gene, were inserted into the *Eco* RI site of pBR322 to create pBH10. Plasmid pBH10 has two *Eco* RI sites and one of these was removed to generate pBH20. Finally, the synthetic somatostatic gene was inserted next to the *lac* control gene to yield pSom I.

The Formation of pBH10 (Fig. 3.6)

Digestion of pBR322 with *Eco* RI produces a linear duplex with short, single-stranded tails. These tails were converted to duplexes by treatment with T4 DNA polymerase to yield a blunt-ended molecule. The endonuclease *Hae* III which produces blunt ends, was used to excise the *lac* control region from bacteriophage λ*plac*. With the aid of T4 DNA ligase, which permits ligation of blunt-ended molecules, the *lac* control region was joined to the blunt ended pBR322 derivative. It should be noted that this procedure results in the formation of two *Eco* RI sites, one on either side of the *lac* control region.

After ligation, the mixture was transformed into *E. coli* and selection made for blue colonies on medium containing ampicillin, tetracycline and the chromogenic substrate 5-bromo-4-chloro-3-indolyl-β-D-galactoside (Xgal). The rationale for this was as follows. Xgal is not an inducer of β-galactosidase but is cleaved by β-galactosidase releasing a blue indolyl derivative. Since Xgal is not an inducer, only mutants constitutive for β-galactosidase produce blue colonies on medium containing Xgal. Plasmid pBH10 is maintained as a relaxed plasmid, i.e. multiple copies per cell. Thus, cells carrying pBH10 have multiple copies of the *lac* control

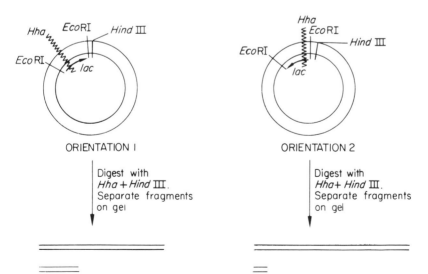

Fig. 3.7 Determination of the orientation of the insert in pBH10 by double digestion with *Hha* and *Hind* III. Note particularly the size of the smallest DNA fragment produced in each case.

region and can titrate out all the repressor produced by the single chromosomal
lac i gene leading to a constitutive phenotype.

Clearly there are two possible orientations for the insertion of the
Hae III fragment but these can be distinguished by the location of an
asymmetrically placed *Hha* site relative to the *Hind* III site (Fig. 3.7).

The Formation of pBH20 (Fig. 3.8)

Plasmid pBH10 has two *Eco* RI sites and it was desirable to retain only
one of them, that located between the *lac* control region and the Tc^R gene.
The *lac* and Tc^R promoters in pBH10 are only 40 base pairs apart and
addition of RNA polymerase effectively protects this site from *Eco* RI

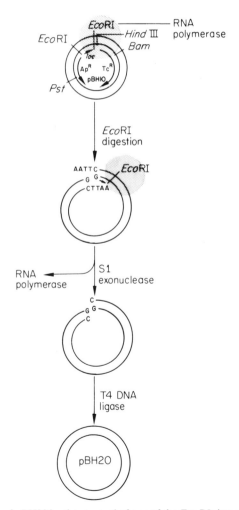

Fig. 3.8   The formation of pBH20 by the removal of one of the *Eco* RI sites of pBH10.

digestion. This is because in the absence of ribonucleotide triphosphates the RNA polymerase does not initiate transcription and remains firmly bound to the promoters. The second *Eco* RI site, however, is exposed. After addition of RNA polymerase, pBH10 was cleaved with *Eco* RI and the single-stranded tails removed with S1 exonuclease. The linear duplex so produced was circularized with T4 DNA ligase to generate pBH20.

The Formation of pSom I (Fig. 3.9)

Plasmid pBH20 was digested with a mixture of *Eco* RI and *Bam* HI to produce a large and small DNA fragment. The small fragment was discarded and the large fragment treated with alkaline phosphatase to prevent subsequent self-ligation (see p. 18). T4 ligase was then used to join the synthetic somatostatin gene to the large fragment of pBH20 and trans-formants were selected by virtue of their ampicillin resistance.

The DNA sequence of pSom I indicated that the clone carrying this plasmid should produce a peptide containing somatostatin, but no somato-statin was found. However, in reconstruction experiments it was observed that exogenous somatostatin was degraded rapidly in *E. coli* extracts. Thus the failure to find somatostatin activity could be accounted for by intra-cellular degradation by endogenous proteolytic enzymes. Such proteolytic degradation might be prevented by attachment of the somatostatin to a large protein, e.g. β-galactosidase. The β-galactosidase structural gene has an *Eco* RI site near the COOH-terminus and the available data on the amino-acid sequence of this protein suggested that it would be possible to insert the synthetic gene into this site and still maintain the proper reading frame. In order to do this, two new plasmids pSom II and pSom II-3 were created.

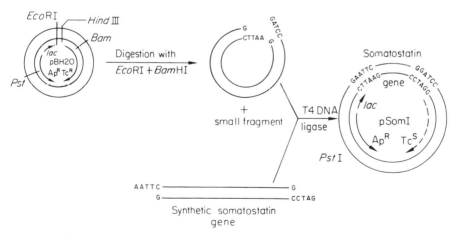

Fig. 3.9 The construction of pSom I by insertion of the synthetic somatostatin gene next to the *lac* control region of pBH20. Note that, for clarity, the step involving alkaline phosphatase (see text) has been omitted.

apparent that such reactions can also occur *in vivo*. Two examples will be presented.

Chang & Cohen (1977) constructed a plasmid, pACYC184, carrying a chloramphenicol-resistance gene with an *Eco* RI site so located that cleavage would inactivate the gene. From pACYC184, plasmid pSC352 was constructed in which the Cm^R gene was inactivated by the insertion of an *Eco* RI fragment of foreign DNA. Transformation of pSC352 into an *E. coli* strain containing the *Eco* RI restriction enzyme resulted in a few transformants (6×10^{-5} of all transformants) which had acquired Cm resistance. *In vitro* analysis showed that such transformants arose from precise excision of the *Eco* RI fragment. In more extensive experiments they showed that *Eco* RI-promoted site-specific recombination could involve multiple and physically separate fragments of plasmid DNA. In each case, however, the plasmids used for transformation were prepared so as to be unmodified against the action of the *Eco* RI restriction enzyme. But what if these sites were already modified? Chang & Cohen thus propagated pSC352 in a strain of *E. coli* where it was modified by the *Eco* RI methylase and then observed the frequency of excision of the inserted fragment under normal growth conditions. Chloramphenicol-resistant colonies developed with a frequency of 10^{-9}. Thus, even the presence of the correct modification enzyme was insufficient to prevent completely site-specific recombination.

Ohsumi *et al.* (1978) have shown that chimaeric DNA molecules can be formed *in vivo* in the absence of a known restriction system. They isolated a recombinant between the filamentous bacteriophage f1 and plasmid pSC101 simply by infecting a pSC101-containing male strain of *E. coli* and selecting for transduction of tetracycline-resistance. The size of the Tc^R-transducing particles and the heteroduplex and restriction enzyme analyses of the replicative form DNA are consistent with the notion that the recombinant contains the entire f1 and pSC101 genomes covalently linked.

Use of Plasmids for Cloning in *Bacillus subtilis*

From the preceding discussion it is clear that plasmids have been used successfully for cloning in *E. coli*. So, why clone in *B. subtilis*? There are a number of reasons for the developing interest in cloning in this organism. Firstly, bacilli are Gram-positive and generally obligate aerobes compared with *E. coli* which is a Gram-negative facultative anaerobe. Thus the two groups of organism may have quite different internal environments. Secondly, *Bacillus* spp. are able to sporulate and consequently are used as models for prokaryotic differentiation. The use of gene manipulation could facilitate these studies. Thirdly, *Bacillus* spp. are widely used in the fermentation industry, particularly for the manufacture of enzymes. Finally, from a biohazard point of view, *Bacillus subtilis* is an extremely safe organism for it has no known interactions with man or other animals. Furthermore, in the literature between 1912 and 1973 there is only one

Table 3.5 *S. aureus* plasmids which function in *B. subtilis*

Plasmid	Resistance markers	Size (Mdal.)	No. of sites for restriction endonuclease							
			Bgl II	*Eco* RI	*Hind* III	*Hpa* II	*Pst* 1	*Sal* 1	*Bam* 1	*Cau* II
pC194	Cm	1.8	0	0	0	1	0	0	1	1
pC221	Cm	3.0	0		1					
pC223	Cm	3.0	0	1	1					
pUB112	Cm	3.0			1					
pT127	Tc	2.9			3					
pE194	Em	2.4	0	0	0	2	1	0	1	
pSA0501	Sm	2.8	0	1	1	2	0	0	1	
pSA2110	Sm, Cm	4.6	0	1	2	3	0	0	1	
pUB110	Km	3.0	1	1	0	4	0	0	1	

transformed *B. subtilis* to chloramphenicol-resistance but the Ap^R gene of pBR322 was not expressed. The failure to get expression of ampicillin-resistance was not due to fragmentation of the hybrid DNA for the *B. subtilis* transformants had acquired plasmids matching those from *E. coli* in both size and *Hind* III restriction pattern. Nor was the lack of expression of the Ap^R gene related to its orientation relative to the pC194 part of the hybrid plasmid because neither pHV14 or pHV15 conferred ampicillin-resistance in *B. subtilis*. The question why the Ap^R gene from *E. coli* is not expressed in *B. subtilis* when the Cm^R gene from *B. subtilis* (originally *S. aureus*) is expressed in *E. coli* is particularly interesting and will be explained more fully in Chapter 7.

Use of Broad Host Range Plasmids as Cloning Vehicles
Plasmids of compatibility group P have uniquely wide host ranges, being able to transfer to and from many bacterial genera. Of the plasmids of this group, RP4 (also called RP1, R1822, R18) is the best studied. RP4 has a mol. wt. of 36×10^6 and single cleavage sites for *Eco* RI, *Bam* HI, *Bgl* II, *Hpa* I and *Hind* III. Relatively little use has been made of RP4 as a cloning vehicle but Jacob *et al.* (1976) have used it for cloning DNA from *Rhizobium leguminosarum* and *Proteus mirabilis*. The recombinant plasmids retained the wide host range of the parental plasmid, were just as efficiently transmitted and were stably maintained in rapidly growing cultures.

Cloning in Yeast (*Saccharomyces cerevisiae*)
The analysis of eukaryotic DNA sequences has been facilitated by the ease with which DNA from eukaryotes can be cloned in prokaryotes using some of the vectors described above. Such cloned sequences can be easily obtained in large amounts and can be altered *in vivo* by bacterial genetic techniques and *in vitro* by specific enzymic modifications. To determine the effects of these experimentally-induced changes on the function and expression of eukaryotic genes, the rearranged sequences must be taken out of the bacteria in which they were cloned and reintroduced into the eukaryotic organism from which they were obtained. Until the recent demonstration of transformation in yeast (Hinnen *et al.* 1978) the latter step was not possible in this organism. Transformation of yeast was achieved by incubating DNA with yeast spheroplasts (i.e. wall-less yeast cells) and then allowing the spheroplasts to regenerate walls in a stabilizing medium containing 3% agar.

The transforming DNA used by Hinnen *et al.* (1978) was plasmid pYeLeu 10 which is a hybrid composed of the *E. coli* plasmid Col E1 and a segment of yeast DNA containing the Leu 2$^+$ gene. Spheroplasts from a stable Leu 2$^-$ auxotroph were transformed to prototrophy by this DNA at a frequency of 1×10^{-7}. Untreated spheroplasts reverted with a frequency of $<1 \times 10^{-10}$. When 42 Leu$^+$ transformants were checked by hybridization,

35 of them contained Col E1 DNA sequences. Genetic analysis of the remaining seven transformants indicated that there had been reciprocal recombination between the incoming Leu 2$^+$ and the recipient Leu 2$^-$ alleles.

Of the 35 transformants containing Col E1 DNA sequences, genetic analysis showed that in 30 of them the Leu 2$^+$ allele was closely linked to the original Leu 2$^-$ allele whereas in the remaining 5, the Leu 2$^+$ allele was located on another chromosome. These results can be confirmed by restriction endonuclease analysis since pYeLeu 10 contains no cleavage sites for *Hind* III. When DNA from the Leu 2$^-$ parent was digested with endonuclease *Hind* III and electrophoresed in agarose, multiple DNA fragments were observed but only one of these hybridized with DNA from pYeLeu 10. With the 30 transformants in which the Leu 2$^-$ and Leu 2$^+$ alleles were linked, only a single fragment of DNA hybridized to pYeLeu 10 but this had an increased size consistent with the insertion of a complete pYeLeu 10 molecule into the original fragment. This data is consistent with their being a tandem duplication of the Leu 2 region of the chromosome (Fig. 3.14). With the remaining five transformants, two DNA fragments which hybridized to pYeLeu 10 could be found on electrophoresis. One fragment corresponded to the fragment seen with DNA from the recipient cells, the other to the plasmid genome which had been inserted in another chromosome (Fig. 3.14). These results represent the first unambiguous demonstration that foreign DNA, in this case Col E1 DNA, can integrate into the genome of a eukaryote.

Struhl *et al.* (1979) have constructed three sets of vectors for cloning

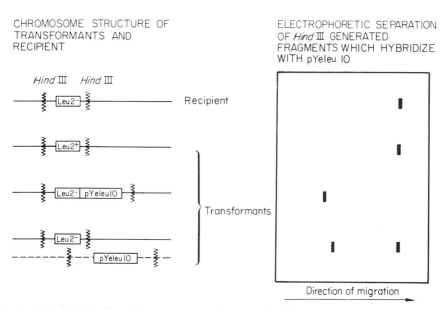

CHROMOSOME STRUCTURE OF
TRANSFORMANTS AND
RECIPIENT

ELECTROPHORETIC SEPARATION
OF *Hind* III GENERATED
FRAGMENTS WHICH HYBRIDIZE
WITH pYeleu 10

Direction of migration

Fig. 3.14 Analysis of yeast transformants. See text for details.

DNA fragments in both yeast and *E. coli.* The first set of vectors contains pBR322 linked to chromosomal DNA sequences and resembles pYeLeu 10 of Hinnen *et al.* (1978). Expression of yeast DNA sequences in yeast requires chromosomal integration of the vector and so transformation frequencies are low (1-10 colonies/μg DNA). The second set of vectors contains endogenous yeast plasmid DNA sequences in addition to yeast chromosomal DNA and pBR322 DNA. Similar vectors derived from pMB9 instead of pBR322 have been described by Beggs (1978). Such vectors transform yeast cells at higher frequencies (5000-20 000 colonies/μg DNA) and this reflects the fact that they can exist in yeast cells in an autonomous or integrated state. The third set of vectors contain a 1.4 Kb yeast DNA fragment which includes the centromere of chromosome IV. These vectors transform with efficiency of 500-5000 colonies/μg DNA and in yeast cells behave as mini-chromosomes. They do not integrate into the genome.

For some time now it has been recognized that gene expression in eukaryotes may well be regulated in different ways from those operating in prokaryotes. Thus the ability to clone DNA in a eukaryote, even if it is a eukaryotic microbe, opens up exciting new avenues for exploration. This aspect of gene manipulation will almost certainly be investigated more fully in the next few years.

Chapter 4. Bacteriophage and Cosmid Vectors

Essential Features of Bacteriophage Lambda [+]

Bacteriophage λ is a genetically complex but very extensively studied virus of *E. coli*. Because it has been the object of so much molecular genetical research it was natural that, right from the beginnings of gene manipulation, it should have been investigated and developed as a vector. The DNA of phage λ, in the form in which it is isolated from the phage particle, is a linear duplex molecule of about 47 Kb pairs. At each end are short single-stranded 5′-projections of 12 nucleotides which are complementary in sequence and by which the DNA adopts a circular structure when it is injected into its host cell, i.e. λ DNA naturally has cohesive termini which associate to form the *cos site*.

Functionally related genes of phage λ are clustered together on the map, except for the two positive regulatory genes *N* and *Q*. Genes on the left of the conventional linear map (Fig. 4.1) code for head and tail proteins of the phage particle. Genes of the central region are concerned with recombination (e.g. *red*) and the process of lysogenization in which the circularized chromosome is inserted into its host chromosome and stably replicated along with it as a prophage. Much of this central region, including these genes, is not essential for phage growth and can be deleted or replaced without seriously impairing the infectious growth cycle. Its dispensability is crucially important, as will become apparent later, in the construction of

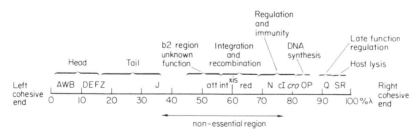

Fig. 4.1 Map of λ chromosome, showing the physical position of some genes on the full length DNA of wild-type bacteriophage λ. Clusters of functionally-related genes are indicated.

[+] Only those features of phage λ that are essential to understanding its use as a vector are discussed here. For a more general account the reader should consult a virology text such as Primrose & Dimmock (1980).

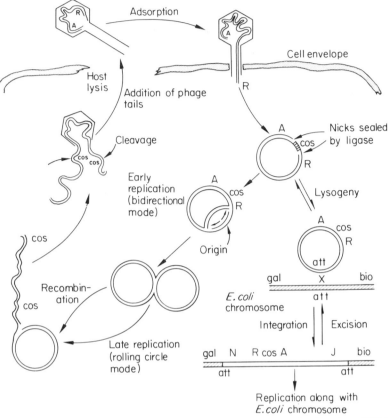

Adsorption

Cell envelope

Host
lysis   Addition of phage
               tails

Cleavage

Early
replication
(bidirectional
mode)

Origin

Recombin-
ation

cos

Late replication
(rolling circle
mode)

Nicks sealed
by ligase

Lysogeny

att

gal   x   bio
E. coli   att
chromosome

Integration | Excision

gal N   R cos A   J   bio
     att   att

Replication along with
E.coli chromosome

Fig. 4.2   Replication of phage λ DNA in lytic and lysogenic cycles. (After Kornberg 1974.)

vector derivatives of the phage. To the right of the central region are genes concerned with gene regulation and prophage immunity to superinfection (*N*, *cro*, *c*I), followed by DNA synthesis (*O*,*P*), late function regulation (*Q*) and host cell lysis (*S*, *R*). Fig. 4.2 illustrates the λ life-cycle.

Promoters and Control Circuits

As we shall see, it is possible to insert foreign DNA into the chromosome of phage λ derivatives, and in some cases foreign genes can be expressed efficiently via λ promoters. We must therefore briefly consider the promoters and control circuits affecting λ gene expression.

In the lytic cycle, λ transcription occurs in three temporal stages; early, middle and late. Basically, early gene transcription establishes the lytic cycle (in competition with lysogeny); middle gene products replicate and recombine the DNA, and late gene products package this DNA into mature phage particles. Following infection of a sensitive host, early transcription proceeds from major promoters situated immediately to the left (P_L) and

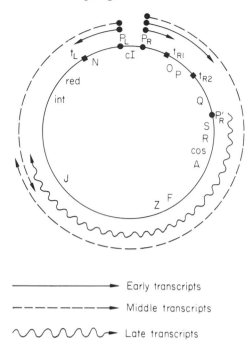

Early transcripts

Middle transcripts

Late transcripts

Fig. 4.3 Major promoters and transcriptional termination sites of phage λ. See text for details.

right (P_R) of the repressor gene (*cI*) (Fig. 4.3). This transcription is subject to repression by the product of the *cI* gene and in a lysogen this repression is the basis of immunity to superinfecting λ. Early in infection transcripts from P_L and P_R stop at termination sites t_L and t_{R1}. The site t_{R2} stops any transcripts that escape beyond t_{R1}. Lambda switches from early to middle stage transcription by anti-termination. The *N* gene product, expressed from P_L, directs this switch. It interacts with RNA polymerase and, antagonizing the action of host termination protein ρ, permits it to ignore the stop signals so that P_L and P_R transcripts extend into genes such as *red* and *O* and *P* necessary for the middle stage. The early and middle transcripts and patterns of expression therefore overlap. The *cro* product, when sufficient has accumulated, depresses transcription from P_L and P_R. The gene *Q* is expressed from the distal portion of the extended P_R transcript and is responsible for the middle to late switch. This also operates by anti-termination. The *Q* product specifically anti-terminates the short P'_R transcript, extending it into the late genes, across the cohered *cos* region, so that many mature phage particles are ultimately produced.

Both *N* and *Q* play positive regulatory roles essential for phage growth and plaque formation; but an N^- phage *can* produce a small plaque if the termination site t_{R2} is removed by a small deletion termed *nin* (N independent) as in λN^-*nin*.

Vector DNA

Wild-type λ DNA contains several target sites for most of the commonly used restriction endonucleases and so is not itself suitable as a vector. Derivatives of the wild-type phage have therefore been produced which either have a single target site at which foreign DNA can be inserted (*insertional* vectors), or have a pair of sites defining a fragment which can be removed and replaced by foreign DNA (*replacement* vectors). Since phage λ can accommodate only about 5% more than its normal complement of DNA, vector derivatives are constructed with deletions to increase the space within the genome. The shortest λ DNA molecules that produce plaques of nearly normal size are 25% deleted. Apparently if too much non-essential DNA is deleted from the genome it cannot be packaged into phage particles efficiently. This can be turned to advantage, for if the replaceable fragment of a replacement type vector either is removed by physical separation, or is effectively destroyed by treatment with a second restriction endonuclease that cuts it alone, then the deleted vector genome can give rise to plaque only if a new DNA segment is inserted into it. This amounts to positive selection for recombinant phage carrying foreign DNA.

Many vector derivatives, of both the insertional and replacement types, have been produced by several groups of researchers (e.g. Thomas *et al.* 1974, Murray & Murray 1975, Blattner *et al.* 1977, Leder *et al.* 1977). Most of these vectors have been constructed for use with *Eco* RI or *Hind* III, but their application can be extended to other endonucleases by the use of linker molecules.

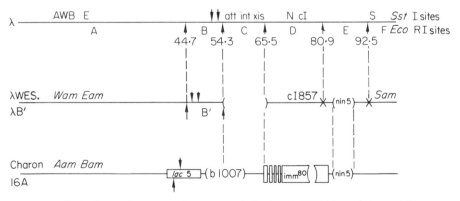

Fig. 4.4   Physical map of λ DNA and two vector derivatives, λWES.λB ′ and charon 16A. Boxes indicate substitutions, but the lengths of substituted DNA are not exactly to scale. The λ regions are aligned. *Lac* 5 is a substitution from the *lac* region of *E. coli*. The box labelled *imm* 80 is a portion of phage φ80 DNA containing its immunity region. The region including four small boxes is derived from φ80 and is partially homologous to λ. Parentheses indicate deletions. Downward and upward arrows are *Sst* I and *Eco* RI restriction sites respectively. Numbers under *Eco* RI sites indicate the positions of the sites as percentages of the wild-type genome length.

The λWES.λB′ phage is a useful vector that illustrates several important points. For details of the construction of this phage the reader is referred to papers of Thomas *et al.* (1974) and Leder *et al.* (1977). The DNA map of this vector is shown in Fig. 4.4. We can see that the phage has been constructed with three amber mutations in genes *W*, *E* and *S*. These reduce the likelihood of recombinants escaping from the laboratory environment since appropriate amber suppressor strains are very uncommon in nature (see Chapter 10). The fragment designated C in wild-type λ has been deleted by restriction and religation *in vitro*. In addition, the two most righthand *Eco* RI sites have been eliminated and a *nin* deletion introduced. The deletions create space for insertion of foreign DNA. The B′ fragment is the replaceable fragment. (The B fragment has inadvertently been inverted during construction of the vector and is designated B′.) In use, the vector DNA is digested with *Eco* RI, then the B′ fragment may be removed by preparative gel electrophoresis or other physical methods. Alternatively, this fragment can be destroyed by treatment of the *Eco* RI digest with *Sst* I. The *Eco* RI-treated foreign DNA is then added to a mixture of vector arms, the mixture is ligated and used to transfect an appropriate amber suppressor strain of *E. coli* so that viable recombinant phage are recovered. Joining of the two DNA arms without insertion of foreign DNA results in a molecule that is too short (9.6% (B′ fragment) + 11.2% (C fragment) + 6.1% (*nin* deletion) = 26.9% less than λ⁺) to produce viable phage even though it contains all of the genes necessary for lytic growth.

Fig. 4.4 also shows the map of one of a set of 16 vector phages constructed by Blattner *et al.* (1977). These have been aptly called Charon phages by their originators, after the old ferryman of Greek mythology who conveyed the spirits of the dead across the River Styx. Some of the Charon phages, like the one illustrated, have had amber mutations introduced in genes *A* and *B* in order to enhance biological containment. Charon 16A is an insertional vector with a single *Eco* RI site located in the gene for β-galactosidase (*lac* Z) which is included in the *lac* 5 DNA substitution. This is useful because there is a convenient colour test for the production of β-galactosidase. When the chromogenic substrate Xgal (see p. 35) is included in the plating medium, phage carrying *lac* 5 give dark blue plaques on Lac⁻ indicator bacteria. Potential success with Charon 16A cloning is detected by insertional inactivation of the Lac function which results in colourless plaques.

Another useful screening method employing insertional inactivation has been exploited by Murray *et al.* (1977). Insertion of foreign DNA at the single target within the immunity region of one of their vector molecules destroys the ability of the phage to produce a functional repressor so that recombinants give clear plaques which are readily distinguished from the turbid plaques of parental phages formed by simple rejoining of the two fragments of the vector DNA.

Expression of Genes Cloned in λ Vectors

It is sometimes the aim of a gene manipulator to promote the expression of a gene which has been cloned so as to amplify the synthesis of a desirable gene product. There is much interest in improving the production of bacterial enzymes that are useful reagents in nucleic acid biochemistry itself—DNA ligase, DNA polymerase and restriction endonucleases are examples that come to mind readily. Panasenko *et al.* (1977) have described a recombinant phage, constructed *in vitro,* carrying the *E. coli* DNA ligase gene which, after induction of the recombinant lysogen, results in a five hundredfold overproduction of the enzyme so that it represent 5% of the total cellular protein of *E. coli.* Dramatic amplification depends *inter alia* upon both increasing the gene dosage and ensuring efficient transcription. The gene dosage is increased as a result of phage DNA replication within the host; the level of transcription may be improved by suitable choice of vector and subsequent manipulation of the recombinant phage.

A great deal of our knowledge about expression of genes cloned in phage λ comes from the studies of N. E. Murray, W. J. Brammar and their colleagues on a model system in which genes from the *trp* operon of *E. coli* are inserted in the phage genome either by manipulation *in vitro* or by genetic methods *in vivo* (Hopkins *et al.* 1976, Moir & Brammar 1976). The following discussion is based on their work.

Firstly, we must distinguish between cases where the inserted DNA does or does not include the bacterial *trp* promoter. If the insert *does* include its own promoter, the yield of *trp* enzymes can be enhanced simply by delaying cell lysis so that the number of gene copies is increased and the time available for expression is extended. This was originally achieved by making the vector S⁻. Moir & Brammar obtained better amplification of gene products by including mutations in gene Q or N. In Q^- phage all the late functions, including that of S, are blocked, and in addition, packaging of the replicated DNA is prevented which even further extends the availability of the DNA. An N^- phage is also defective in late functions and although it replicates more slowly than N^+Q^- phage, yields of enzyme achieved were at least as great. In such infected cells anthranilate synthetase, the product of *trp E* and *D* genes, comprised more than 25% of the total soluble protein.

λ *trp* phage *lacking* the *trp* promoter have been constructed so that *trp* expression is initiated at the promoter P_L of the leftward operon of phage λ. This operon has two useful features:
(1) P_L is a powerful promoter;
(2) the anti-termination effect of gene N expression permits transcription through sequences which might otherwise prevent expression of a distant inserted gene.
Once again, cell lysis and DNA packaging were prevented by mutations in Q and S and additionally, the *cro⁻* mutation was introduced so as to derepress transcription from P_L. Cells infected with such a phage may

contain as much as 10% of the soluble protein as anthranilate synthetase. However, these phage were difficult to construct and propagate so an alternative approach was adopted. The *cro* gene lies within the immunity region and its product is immune-specific. The *cro* product of the hetero-immune phage 434 will not interact with P_L of λ. Hybrid phage containing P_L from λ but *cro* and P_R from 434 are therefore phenotypically Cro⁻ as far as leftward transcription is concerned. Infection with such a λ*trp* derivative, which also carried the S^- mutation, gave cells in which 25% of the soluble protein was anthranilate synthetase. Derivatives of this type which are *N*am can be grown on a non-suppressing host providing they also carry the *nin* deletion of t_{R2}. Thus amplification can be modulated by controlling the suppression of the *N*am gene. This is a useful property since extreme over-production of a product relaxes the selection that can be imposed on a recombinant clone and may lead to problems of instability.

This elegant exploitation of the genetics of phage λ demonstrates the advantages of a well characterized genetic system and encourages the hope that useful amplification of a variety of gene products may be achieved with λ vectors, even in cases where a strong promoter, recognized by the host RNA polymerase, does not accompany the inserted gene.

Packaging phage λ DNA *in vitro*

So far, we have considered only one way of introducing manipulated phage DNA into the host bacterium, i.e. by transfection of competent bacteria (see Chapter 1). Using freshly prepared λ DNA that has not been subjected to any gene manipulation procedures, transfection will result in typically about 10^5 plaques per microgram of DNA. In a gene manipulation experiment in which the vector DNA is restricted etc., and then ligated with foreign DNA, this figure is reduced to about 10^4-10^3 plaques per microgram of vector DNA. Even with perfectly efficient nucleic acid biochemistry some of this reduction is inevitable. It is a consequence of the random association of fragments in the ligation reaction which produces molecules with a variety of fragment combinations, many of which are inviable. Yet, in some contexts, 10^6 or more recombinants are required. The scale of such experiments can be kept within a reasonable limit (less than 100 μg vector DNA) by packaging the recombinant DNA into mature phage particles *in vitro*.

Placing the recombinant DNA in a phage coat then allows it to be introduced into the host bacteria by the normal processes of phage infection, i.e. phage adsorption followed by DNA injection. Depending upon the details of the experimental design, packaging *in vitro* yields about 10^6 plaques per microgram of vector DNA after the ligation reaction.

Fig. 4.5 shows some of the events occurring during the packaging process that take place within the host during normal phage growth and which we now require to perform *in vitro*. Phage DNA in concatemeric form,

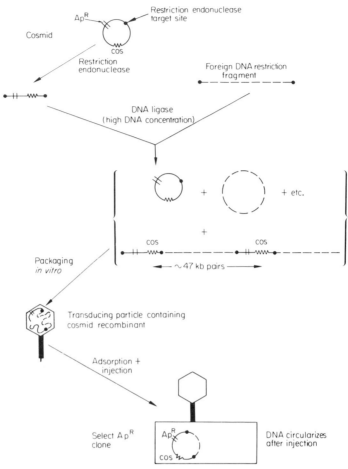

Fig. 4.6   Scheme for cloning in a cosmid vector. See text for details.

alkaline phosphatase (page 18). Because of their capacity for large fragments
of DNA, cosmids are particularly attractive vectors for constructing
libraries of eukaryotic genome fragments. Partial digestion with restriction
endonuclease provides suitably large fragments.   However, there is a
potential problem associated with the use of partial digests in this way.
This is due to the possibility of two or more genome fragments joining
together in the ligation reaction hence creating a clone containing fragments
that were not initially adjacent in the genome.   Such joined fragments
could be mistaken subsequently for genuine partial digestion products.
The problem can be overcome by careful size-fractionation of the partial
digest. Alternatively, as pointed out by Collins & Brüning (1978), alkaline
phosphatase treatment of the foreign DNA prevents joining of fragments
that were not initially adjacent in the genome. This trick should prove most

useful in the analysis of large eukaryotic genomes. In addition, packaging cosmid recombinants into phage λ coats should allow the use of some genetic procedures previously applicable only to λ. Details of these procedures are beyond the scope of this book, but it is worth mentioning the use of chelating agents to select for deletions (Parkinson & Huskey 1971) and very stringent selection for phage containing DNA of wild-type size or larger by infection of a *pel⁻* host (Emmons *et al.* 1975, Scandella & Arber 1976).

A Phage Vector other than Lambda—M13

The presence of the large non-essential region in the phage λ genome is very useful in constructing vector derivatives. However, another coliphage that has a completely different genome organization and life-cycle—phage M13—has been developed recently as a cloning vector (Messing *et al.* 1977, Barnes 1979).

This filamentous phage contains single-stranded circular DNA, mol. wt. about 2 million, that is converted within the infected cell into a double-stranded replicative form which is amplified to about 300 copies per cell. Cells that produce phage do not lyse but continue to grow and divide. Because growth is retarded by M13 infection, turbid plaques are formed by plating on indicator bacteria. The most useful feature of M13 vectors is the potential for easily preparing cloned foreign DNA in single-stranded form from phage particles. Either strand can be recovered if two clones are constructed with the foreign DNA in opposite orientations. The ready availability of the DNA in single-stranded form greatly facilitates nucleotide sequence determination by certain newly-developed rapid methods (see Air 1979, for review).

M13 does not have a large non-essential region. Amber mutations in almost any gene lead to host killing and hence no virus production. In order to search for a potential non-essential intergenic site, a population of replicative-form molecules each with single cuts per molecule but at many different sites, has been used for *in vitro* DNA insertion. Such a population was produced by very limited digestion with a restriction endonuclease for which the DNA has many target sites. In this way, a fragment of the *lac* regulatory region of *E. coli* has been cloned in M13, as has part of the *his* operon of *Salmonella typhimurium*. In the latter case, the new recombinant was isolated in an *E. coli* histidine auxotroph by selecting for prototrophic growth of host *colonies*. This new recombinant now itself represents an improved cloning vector because of the presence of the histidine marker for selection of transformed colonies and because a new, single, *Eco* RI site was introduced at one boundary of the *his* DNA insert (Barnes 1979).

Although M13 vectors have yet to be exploited very extensively, it is reasonable to expect that they will be used where sequences in single-stranded form are required, and because M13 is a filamentous phage, the presence of relatively large inserts should not interfere with phage morphogenesis.

Not only can DNA be inserted into M13 DNA by *in vitro* manipulation, it can also be inserted *in vivo*. The way this can be done has already been described on page 40 for the closely related phage f1.

Chapter 5. Cloning Strategies

Any DNA cloning experiment has four essential parts: a method for generating DNA fragments; a method for joining the fragments to vector DNA molecules; a means of introducing the composite DNA molecule, the artificial recombinant, into a host cell in which it can replicate; and a method of selecting a clone of recipient cells that has acquired the recombinant. In previous chapters, DNA cutting and joining reactions have been described, and the properties of phage and plasmid vectors have been discussed. What factors govern the choice between the various cutting and joining methods and different vector molecules?

We must consider the nature and purity of the DNA to be cloned. As an example, let us suppose that we wish to clone a single-copy gene from the human genome. We might simply digest total human DNA with a restriction endonuclease such as *Eco* RI, insert these fragments into a suitable plasmid or phage vector and then attempt to select the desired clone. How many clones would we have to screen in the selection procedure? Assuming *Eco* RI (hexanucleotide target site) gives, on average, fragments about 4Kb long, and given that the size of the human haploid genome is 2.8×10^6 Kb, then we can see that over 7×10^5 independent clones must be prepared and screened in order to have a reasonable chance of including the desired sequence.

One difficulty with this approach arises from the possibility that one or more *Eco* RI sites might occur within the desired sequence. We could accept this possibility and attempt to recover several clones that together comprise the whole sequence. If necessary, the entire sequence could later be reconstructed from the cloned fragments. Alternatively, we could seek a restriction endonuclease that has no target site within the sequence. This may not be easy if the desired sequence is a long one—perhaps 35 Kb. In that case, we may wish to prepare a set of random fragments by mechanical shearing; or we could make a *partial* digest with one, or a combination of restriction endonucleases. In either case, fragments in the correct size range could be obtained by size-fractionation on sucrose gradient centrifugation. A cosmid vector would have a suitably large capacity for such long fragments, and *in vitro* packaging into phage coats would provide the means of obtaining the necessary large number (greater than 10^5) of independent clones. This set of clones would be expected to comprise the entire human genome and it is sometimes referred to as a complete *library* or *gene-bank* from which the appropriate selection is made. For obvious reasons, this is sometimes called a *shot-gun* experiment.

As an alternative approach we could obtain a partially purified DNA fraction which is enriched in the desired sequence. The task of selection would be diminished correspondingly. One method that has been employed very successfully for such enrichment is chromatography upon the medium RPC-5 which consists of a quaternary ammonium salt, the extractant, supported upon a matrix of plastic beads. Originally developed for high-resolution reversed phase chromatography of tRNAs, it will fractionate milligram quantities of DNA fragments generated by restriction endonucleases (Hardies & Wells 1976). Leder and his co-workers (Tilghman *et al.* 1977) loaded an *Eco* RI digest of total mouse genomic DNA onto an RPC-5 column, and upon elution with a concentration gradient of sodium acetate, obtained a series of DNA fractions which were assayed for their ability to hybridize with mouse globin cDNA. A fraction was identified as being substantially enriched in a DNA fragment bearing β-globin sequences. The discrimination on the RPC-5 column chromatography is only slightly dependent upon fragment size, so that additional enrichment (to about 500-fold) could be obtained by combining it with preparative gel electrophoresis. The final enriched fraction was ligated into the λWES.λB vector, and out of about 4300 plaques obtained by transfection, 3 positive clones were detected.

Multiple-copy genes, even without prior enrichment, do not, of course, require the screening of so many clones as single-copy genes. In fact, the clustered 5S DNA copies and the extrachromosomal rDNA copies of the frog *Xenopus* are present in so many copies that they can be isolated in pure form on the basis of their buoyant density difference from bulk DNA in centrifugation gradients of caesium salts. Thus these genes can be purified without gene cloning—but with one significant difference. Studies of the non-cloned sequences deal with average properties of the material. It is only by cloning individual copies that microheterogeneity within genes or spacers, down to the nucleotide sequence level, can be investigated.

In the case of cDNA cloning, there is a similar trade-off between cDNA purity and the effort of selection. A general account of mRNA purification is beyond the scope of this book, but the following procedure illustrates how techniques discussed in previous chapters can be ingeniously applied to the purification of a cDNA.

Shine (1977) and his co-workers obtained a polyadenylated mRNA preparation which directed the synthesis of a precursor form of human chorionic somatomammotropin (HCS) when translated in a cell-free system. However they estimated that the preparation was only 50% pure, being contaminated with other mRNA species whose cDNA sequences they did not wish to clone. First, the mRNA was reverse transcribed

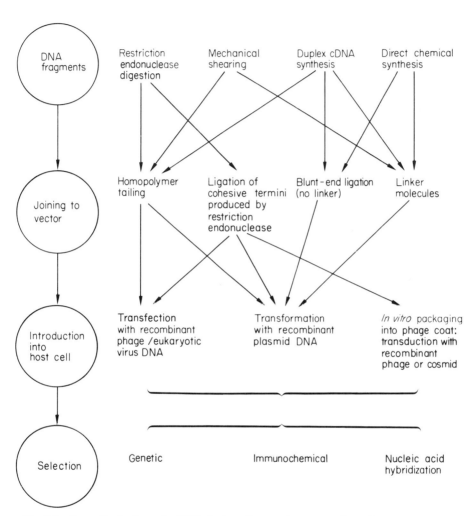

Fig. 5.1 Generalized scheme for DNA cloning. Favoured routes are shown by arrows.

into cDNA which was then converted into duplex cDNA (see Chapter 2). As expected, this duplex cDNA was heterodisperse as judged by gel electrophoresis, but gave rise to a predominant 550-base pair fragment when digested with *Hae* III. This fragment, which was known to be derived from the HCS mRNA, was isolated from the gel, treated with alkaline phosphatase, and cleaved into two fragments with a second restriction endonuclease. The two major cleavage products were then re-isolated by gel electrophoresis. During this step most of the contaminating sequences were removed because they remained uncleaved or were cleaved in a different relative position. The two isolated fragments were then religated to form the original fragment. The previous treatment of the original 550-base pair fragment with alkaline phosphatase ensured that these two fragments were capable of ligation to each other only in the correct orientation, although self-ligation to form dimers was also possible. Isolation of the original fragment, reconstructed by religation of its constituent digestion products, resulted in a pure DNA species which was then cloned in pMB9 using chemically-synthesized linker molecules.

In general, the choice of fragment-to-vector joining procedure will depend upon such factors as:

(1) simplicity;
(2) possible need to produce joints which can be cleaved for re-isolation of the foreign sequence;
(3) influence upon transcriptional or translational read-through (see Chapter 7).

The choice of vector will depend upon factors in addition to biological containment, such as:

(1) capacity for long foreign DNA fragments;
(2) applicability of amplification by chloramphenicol treatment (plasmids);
(3) required host range (promiscuous plasmids);
(4) applicability of insertional inactivation or other selection for insertion events;
(5) availability of vector-borne promoter (see Chapters 2, 3 and 7).

Newly-created recombinant DNA can be introduced into the host cell by transformation (plasmid DNA) or transfection (phage DNA). Where large numbers of clones are required, *in vitro* packaging of either phage or cosmid recombinants may be favoured. The choice of a suitable selection method is considered in the following chapter.

At the start of this chapter four separate parts of any gene cloning experiment were listed. Fig. 5.1 shows how the different ways of accomplishing each part of the experiment can be combined to form a feasible plan. In summary, we can see that the plan adopted must depend upon the nature and purity of the starting material, as well as upon the foreseen application of the clones that are ultimately obtained.

Chapter 6. Recombinant Selection and Characterization

The task of selecting a desired recombinant from a population of transformed, transfected or transduced bacteria depends very much upon the cloning strategy that has been adopted. For instance, when a cDNA derived from a purified mRNA is to be cloned the task is relatively simple; only a small number of clones need to be screened in order to select the required clone. Selecting a particular single-copy gene sequence amongst all the recombinants of a mammalian shot-gun gene cloning procedure is more demanding.

The purpose of this chapter is to outline important methods that have been applied to the selection and ultimate characterization of recombinant clones. It is not an exhaustive account; variations on these themes will no doubt occur to the thoughtful reader, and particular experimental systems will sometimes present special opportunities that can be turned to advantage.

Genetic Methods

(i) *Selection for Presence of Vector*
When combined with microbiological techniques, genetic selection is a very powerful tool since it can be applied to large populations.

All useful vector molecules carry a selectable genetic marker or have a genetically selectable property. Plasmid vectors carry drug resistance or nutritional markers, and in the case of phage vectors, plaque formation itself is the selectable property. Genetic selection for presence of the vector is the first stage in obtaining the recombinant population of cells. As we have seen previously, this selection can be refined. For example, insertional inactivation or size-dependent selection can be used to distinguish recombinant molecules and nonrecombinant parental vector (see pages 33 and 50).

(ii) *Selection of Inserted Sequences*
If an inserted foreign gene in the desired recombinant is expressed, then genetic selection may provide the simplest method for isolating clones containing the gene. Cloned *E. coli* DNA fragments carrying biosynthetic genes can be identified by complementation of nonrevertable auxotrophic mutations in the host *E. coli* strain. A related example comes from the work of Cameron *et al.* (1975) who have cloned the *E. coli* DNA ligase gene

in a phage λgt.λB vector. They exploited the inability of λ*red*⁻ phage (the vector is *red*⁻ by deletion of the C fragment) to form plaques on *E. coli lig* ts at the permissive temperature, whereas λ*red*⁻ phage will form plaques on *E. coli* Lig⁺. Recombinant phage carrying the wild-type ligase function could therefore be selected simply by their ability to form plaques through complementation of the host deficiency when plated on *E. coli lig* ts.

It has been found that certain eukaryotic genes are expressed in *E. coli* and can complement auxotrophic mutations in the host bacterium. Ratzkin & Carbon (1977) inserted fragments of yeast DNA, obtained by mechanical shearing, into the plasmid Col E1 using a homopolymer tailing procedure. They transformed *E. coli his* B mutants with recombinant plasmid and, by selecting for complementation, isolated clones carrying an expressed yeast *his* gene.

A similar approach has even been applied successfully to cloned mouse sequences. Chang *et al.* (1978) constructed a population of recombinant plasmids containing cDNA that was derived from an unfractionated mouse cell mRNA preparation in which dihydrofolate reductase (DHFR) mRNA was present. Mouse DHFR is much less sensitive to inhibition by the drug trimethoprim than is *E. coli* DHFR, so that by selecting transformants in medium containing the drug, clones were isolated in which resistance was conferred by synthesis of the mouse enzyme. This was an early example of expression of a mammalian structural gene in *E. coli*. The factors affecting expression of heterologous genes are complex, and an efficient selection procedure was required in order to identify clones actually synthesizing mouse DHFR amongst those containing non-expressed DHFR cDNA (see Chapter 7).

Immunochemical Methods

Immunochemical detection of clones synthesizing a foreign protein has also been successful in cases where the inserted gene sequence is expressed. A particular advantage of the method is that genes which do not confer any selectable property on the host can be detected, but it does of course require that specific antibody is available.

A number of laboratories have developed similar immunochemical detection methods (Skalka & Shapiro 1976, Ehrlich *et al.* 1978). The method of Broome & Gilbert (1978) has been applied most widely. It depends upon three points.

(1) An immune serum contains several IgG types that bind to different determinants on the antigen molecule;
(2) Antibody molecules adsorb very strongly to plastics such as polyvinyl, from which they are not removed by washing;
(3) IgG antibody can be readily radiolabelled with ¹²⁵I by iodination *in vitro*.

These properties are elegantly exploited in the following way. First, transformed colonies are plated on agar in a conventional petri dish. A replica plate must also be prepared because subsequent procedures kill these colonies. The bacterial colonies are then lysed in one of a number of ways—by exposure to chloroform vapour; by spraying with an aerosol of virulent phage; or by using a host bacterium that carries a thermo-inducible prophage. This releases the antigen from positive colonies. A sheet of polyvinyl that has been coated with the appropriate antibody (unlabelled) is applied to the surface of the plate, whereupon the antigen complexes with the bound IgG. The sheet is removed and exposed to ^{125}I-labelled IgG. The ^{125}-I-IgG can react with the bound antigen via antigenic determinants at sites other than those involved in the initial binding of antigen to the IgG-coated sheet, as shown in Fig. 6.1. Positively-reacting colonies are detected by washing the sheet and making an autoradiographic image. The required clones can then be recovered from the replica plate. The method can, of course, be applied, with only minor modification, to plates bearing phage plaques instead of transformed colonies.

Two further aspects of the method deserve mention. Firstly, detection of altered protein molecules is possible providing that the alteration does not prevent cross-reaction with antibody. Thus Villa-Komaroff *et al.* (1978) have isolated *E. coli* clones containing cDNA sequences from rat prepro-insulin mRNA. The cDNA was inserted by dG-dC homopolymer tailing at the *Pst* I site of pBR322. Using anti-insulin antibody, they isolated a clone which expressed a fused protein composed of the N-terminal region of β-lactamase (from pBR322) and a region of the proinsulin protein linked

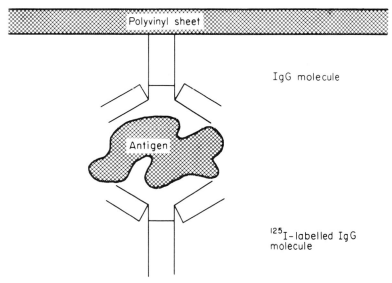

Fig. 6.1 Antigen-antibody complex formation in the immunochemical detection method of Broome & Gilbert. (See text for details.)

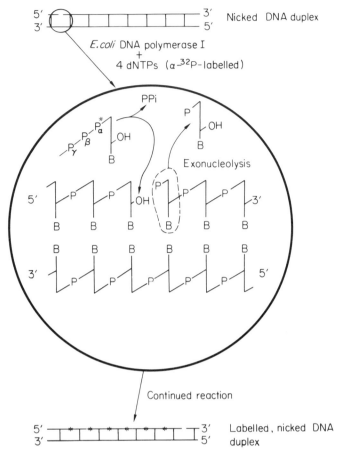

Fig. 6.3 ^{32}P-labelling of duplex DNA by nick-translation. Asterisks indicate radiolabelled phosphate groups.

a free 3′-OH group, DNA polymerase 1 of *E. coli* will incorporate nucleotides successively. Concomitant hydrolysis of the 5′-terminus by the 5′→3′ exonucleolytic activity of polymerase 1 releases 5′-mononucleotides. If the four deoxynucleoside triphosphates are radiolabelled (e.g. α-^{32}P-dNTPs), the reaction progressively incorporates the label into a duplex that is unchanged except for translation of the nick along the molecule. Because the original nicking occurs virtually at random, a DNA preparation is effectively labelled uniformly to a degree depending upon the extent of nucleotide replacement and specific radioactivity of the labelled precursors. Often the reaction is performed with only one of the four deoxynucleoside triphosphates in labelled form. In that case, non-uniform base composition, especially homopolymer stretches, will lead to a non-uniform pattern of labelling which may affect subsequent applications.

Characterization of Recombinant DNA

Once a recombinant carrying a DNA sequence of particular interest has been isolated it is necessary to characterize the DNA further. This may simply extend so far as confirming that the required DNA has indeed been cloned, or as is often the case, the complete characterization of the DNA, including nucleotide sequencing, may be the ultimate aim of the cloning experiment.

When a recombinant DNA has been newly isolated, its size can be determined by gel electrophoresis. If the vector is a plasmid replicating under relaxed control, sufficient copies are present in host bacteria for it to be unnecessary to purify the plasmid DNA prior to electrophoresis. Single bacterial colonies from an agar plate can be picked, lysed in a small volume by treatment with hot sodium dodecyl sulphate, and then loaded directly onto an agarose gel. After electrophoresis, the gel can be stained with ethidium bromide to clearly reveal plasmid bands separated from the bulk of host DNA (Barnes 1977, Telford *et al.* 1977). The 'single colony lysate' method is so simple that it can be applied as a preliminary screen to a large number of isolates if required (Fig. 6.4). The restriction map of inserted foreign DNA may help to identify the cloned sequence, and, in any case, is indispensable if detailed characterization is to be carried out.

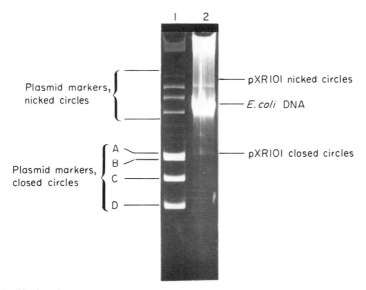

Fig. 6.4 Single colony lysate method applied to a recombinant plasmid. Electrophoresis track 1 shows a mixture of purified plasmid marker DNAs. A, 12.7 Mdal; B, 11.5 Mdal; C, 9.6 Mdal. Plasmid marker D is pCR1, 8.5 Mdal. Track 2 shows a single colony lysate containing pXR101 DNA which was constructed by inserting a 4.2 Mdal fragment of *Xenopus laevis* ribosomal DNA into the pCR1 vector. The recombinant plasmid DNA, in either nicked or closed circular form, is resolved from the broad band of *E. coli* (host) DNA. (Photograph courtesy of Dr. P. Boseley.)

of distinct abundant polypeptides that can be resolved on 2-dimensional electrophoresis systems. It should be quite feasible to isolate recombinant cDNAs derived from such a mixed population of mRNAs, and correlate them with their corresponding polypeptides.

R-loop Mapping

RNA can hybridize to *double-stranded DNA* by displacing the identical DNA strand (Fig. 6.5). The resulting structure is called an R-loop (Thomas *et al.* 1976, White & Hogness 1977). The formation of R-loops requires careful control of reaction conditions and depends upon the greater stability of the RNA-DNA hybrid in 70% formamide near the denaturation temperature of duplex DNA. Once formed, R-loops are quite stable and can be observed in the electron microscope whereby they can be used to map the region in a DNA duplex that is homologous to a given RNA (see Fig. 6.6).

The observed topographies of R-loops formed between cloned eukaryotic genome fragments and corresponding mRNA or rRNA have shown that many eukaryotic genes consist of non-contiguous coding regions split by one or more *intervening sequences* or *introns*.

Chapter 7. Expression of Cloned DNA Molecules

Following the demonstration (see page 29) that a gene (Ap^R) originating from *Staphylococcus aureus* can function in an unrelated bacterium, *Escherichia coli*, it was widely assumed that genes from any bacterium could be expressed in any other. This belief was based on the expectation that, in parallel with the universality of the genetic code, the other parts of the gene-to-phenotype biochemical pathway would also be universal. This idea was strengthened by the observation that genes from two lower eukaryotes, *Saccharomyces cerevisiae* (Struhl *et al.* 1976) and *Neurospora crassa* (Vapnek *et al.* 1977) are also expressed in *E. coli*. For that reason the genes from higher organisms were also expected to be expressed in bacteria. However, in recent years a growing number of reports (Table 7.1) in the literature have indicated that not all cloned DNA molecules are expressed in their new genetic background.

Table 7.1 Examples, taken from published reports, of cloned DNA sequences which were not expressed in *E. coli*. It should not be assumed that inclusion of a DNA sequence in this list means that gene expression has not been obtained subsequently.

DNA cloned	Comments
Streptomyces spp.	No complementation of Met-, Thi-, Pro- *E. coli* auxotrophs
Silk fibroin cDNA	No translation reported
Sea urchin histone genes	No translation reported
Globin cDNA (from various sources)	No translation reported
Chick ovalbumin cDNA	No translation reported
Mouse immunoglobulin cDNA	No translation reported
Rat insulin cDNA	No translation reported

Synthesis of a functional protein depends upon transcription of the appropriate gene, efficient translation of the mRNA and, in many cases, post-translational processing and compartmentalization of the nascent polypeptide. A failure to perform correctly any one of these processes can result in the failure of a given gene to be expressed. Transcription of a cloned insert requires the presence of a promoter recognized by the host RNA polymerase. Efficient translation requires that the mRNA bears a ribosome binding site. In the case of an *E. coli* mRNA a ribosome binding site includes the translational start codon (AUG or GUG) and another sequence that is complementary to bases on the 3′ end of 16S ribosomal RNA. Shine & Dalgarno (1975) first postulated the requirement for this homology, and various S-D sequences, as they are often called, have been found in almost all *E. coli* mRNAs examined. Identified S-D sequences vary in length from 3-9 bases and precede the translational start codon by 3-12 bases (Steitz 1979). A common post-translational modification of proteins involves cleavage of a *signal* sequence whose function is to direct the passage of the protein through the cell membrane (Blobel & Doberstein 1975, Inouye & Beckwith 1977). Another phenomenon, possibly related to the processing of proteins, is their degradation. It is known that the short polypeptides encoded by genes which have undergone nonsense mutations are rapidly degraded in *E. coli* while the wild-type proteins are stable. It can be envisaged that the foreign proteins would be rapidly degraded in the new host if their configuration or amino acid sequence did not protect them from intracellular proteases.

Construction of Vectors which Give Improved Transcription of Inserts

From the above discussion it is clear that the first requirement for expression in *E. coli* of a structural gene, inserted *in vitro* in a DNA molecule, is that the gene be placed under the control of an *E. coli* promoter. For this purpose, Fuller (see Backmann *et al.* 1976) has constructed a 'portable promoter' in the form of a DNA fragment known as *Eco*RI (UV5). This fragment carries the regulatory region of the *lac* operon and the UV5 mutation bounded by *Eco*RI generated cohesive ends. The fragment also carries the L8 mutation but this does not affect its use. The L8 mutation is only mentioned here for the sake of completeness and to avoid confusion when reading the literature. The UV5 mutation makes the system insensitive to catabolite repression. One of the *Eco*RI sites is located 65 base pairs downstream from the start point of transcription, a position corresponding to the ninth amino acid residue of the *lac* Z gene. Backmann *et al.* (1976) have constructed a plasmid in which this *Eco*RI (UV5) fragment is fused to the repressor gene (cI) of bacteriophage λ. Strains carrying this plasmid overproduced the λ repressor and *transcription* of the cI gene was largely under *lac* control.

Charnay *et al.* (1979) have engineered the *Eco*RI (UV5) fragment onto λ by insertion at the single *Eco*RI site of λ *plac* 5.1. This gives recombinant phage carrying two *lac* regulatory regions. There are two consequences of this insertion. Firstly, the recombinant phage should be Lac⁻. Secondly, there are two possible orientations of the insert but one of them gives molecules which undergo intramolecular recombination resulting in the removal of the greater part of the *lac* z gene (Fig. 7.1). Recombinant phage

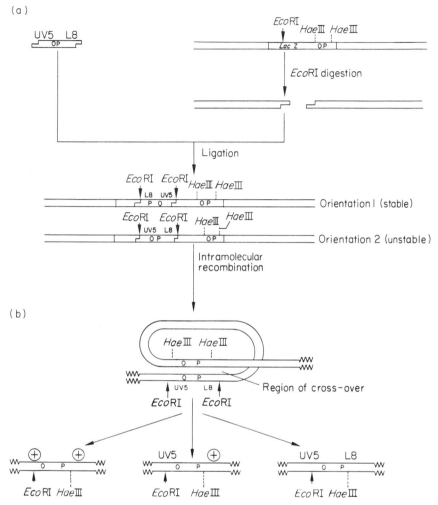

Fig. 7.1   The construction of λΔZ UV5. (A) The insertion of the *Eco* RI (UV5) fragment into the *Eco* RI site of *plac* 5.1. (B) Enlarged view of the intramolecular recombination events which lead to the formation of λΔZ UV5.

were selected on the basis of their Lac⁻ phenotype and titred on Lac⁺ bacteria using Xgal medium (page 35). As expected, two kinds of phage were observed. The first gave between 5 and 100% colourless plaques on Xgal, while the other gave only blue plaques.   Phage of the first type could have one of three phenotypes depending on the position of the recombination event (Fig. 7.1). Because the presence of the UV5 mutation on the *lac* promoter introduces insensitivity to catabolite repression, recombinants carrying the UV5 mutation were selected. Such recombinants are called λΔZ UV5.

An important feature of λΔZ UV5 phages is that they have only a single

*Eco*RI site, the one originally located on the *Eco*RI (UV5) fragment downstream from the *lac* promoter. Mercerau-Puijalon *et al.* (1978) have now transposed the *lac* control region from λΔZ UV5 to pBR322 to create a new plasmid called pOMPO. This was done very simply by digesting λΔZ UV5 and pBR322 with a combination of *Eco*RI and *Hind*III, ligating the mixture and selecting transformants with the right phenotype (Ap^{R}Tc^s colonies which are blue on Xgal medium). As outlined below, pOMPO has been used to obtain expression of a cloned cDNA transcript of ovalbumin mRNA.

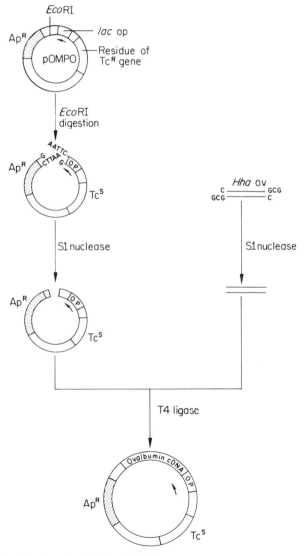

Fig. 7.2 Cloning of ovalbumin cDNA in pOMPO.

Ovalbumin cDNA had already been cloned in a plasmid and could be isolated from this plasmid as a *Hha*I restriction fragment (called *Hha* ov) of 2430 base pairs. This fragment was digested with S1 nuclease to produce blunt ends and ligated to *Eco*RI digested pOMPO which had been similarly treated (Fig. 7.2). Provided the *Hha* ov fragment is inserted in the proper orientation, such hybrids should produce an ovalbumin-like protein of 389 amino acids, instead of 386, in which the first 5 amino acids of ovalbumin are substituted by the first 8 amino acids of β-galactosidase (Fig. 7.3). Approximately half of the recombinants could be shown by restriction mapping to have the *Hha* fragment in the right orientation, and following transformation into *E. coli* produced an ovalbumin-like product detectable by radioimmunoassay. The remaining recombinants had the cDNA in the wrong orientation and failed to produce material reacting with anti-ovalbumin antibodies.

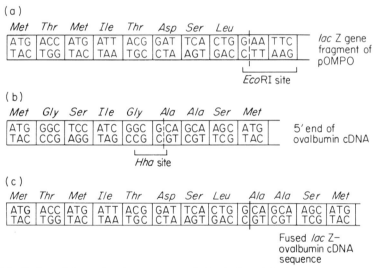

Fig. 7.3 Fusion of the ovalbumin sequence to the beginning of the *lac* Z gene. The DNA sequence of the *Eco* RI restricted *lac* Z gene fragment is shown in (A). The first eight amino acids of ovalbumin and their corresponding DNA sequence are shown in (B). Elimination of the single-stranded ends and blunt-end ligation produce the fused gene sequence shown in (C). The broken lines indicate the position of the flush-ends produced after S1 nuclease treatment. The solid vertical line indicates the position of the joint between the *lac* Z and ovalbumin sequences.

Positioning Cloned Inserts in the Correct Translational Reading Frame

The successful expression in *E. coli* of the cloned ovalbumin gene was dependent on the maintenance of the correct translational reading frame following its fusion to the *lac* Z gene. Clearly, with many other genes adjustment might have to be made at the gene junction in order to maintain the correct translational phase. In order to avoid this adjustment for each particular case, Charnay *et al.* (1978) constructed a set of vectors, each having a single *Eco*RI restriction site, in which the cloned gene can be placed in each of the three possible reading frames relative to the translation initiation site of the *lac* Z gene. A DNA fragment inserted at the *Eco*RI site of λΔZ UV5 (described above) is in the reading frame arbitrarily defined as $\phi1$. λΔZ vectors in which the inserted fragments can be positioned in phases $\phi2$ and $\phi3$ (λΔZ2 and λΔZ3) were constructed by two successive additions of 2G-C base pairs to each end of the *Eco*RI (UV5) fragment (Fig. 7.4).

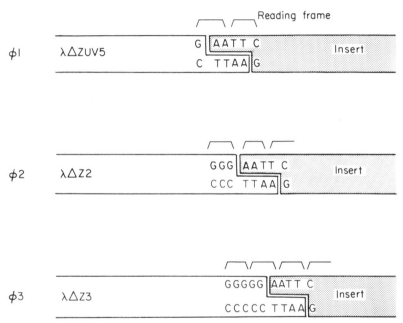

Fig. 7.4 The different reading frames with respect to the translation initiation site of the *lac* Z gene presented by the three λ vectors.

The procedure for adding 2 base pairs to each end of the 203 base pair *Eco*RI (UV5) fragment is shown in Fig. 7.5. The fragment was treated with S1 nuclease in order to produce flush ends with G-C as the final base pair. Using T4 ligase a synthetic *Eco*RI linker was then attached to each end of the fragment and this was followed by digestion with *Eco*RI endonuclease. This resulted in the production of a 207 base pair fragment called *Eco*RI 207 (UV5). Using the same procedure, *Eco*RI 207 (UV5) was converted to *Eco*RI 211 (UV5). Both the 207 and 211 base pair fragments were then inserted into λ *plac* 5.1 by the method shown in Fig. 7.1, to produce λΔZ2 and λΔZ3. These fragments were also transferred to pBR322 by the method of Mercerau-Puijalon *et al.* (1978) as outlined above.

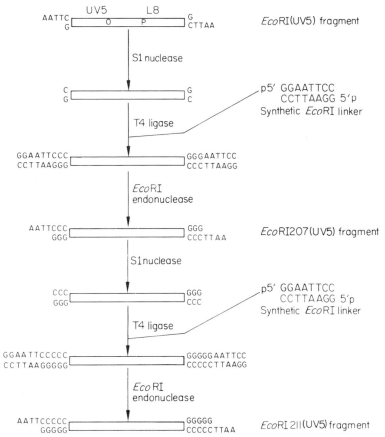

Fig. 7.5 Construction of the *Eco* RI 211 (UV5) fragment by two successive additions of two G-C base pairs to each end of the *Eco* RI (UV5) fragment.

An Alternative Strategy: Cloning in the *Pst*I Site of pBR322

An alternative method of putting an insert under the control of an *E. coli* promoter without the concomitant problem of translational reading frame adjustment has been used by Villa-Komaroff *et al.* (1978). They cloned cDNA transcripts of rat preproinsulin mRNA at the unique *Pst*I site of pBR322 (see Fig. 3.4). This site lies in the Ap^R gene at a position corresponding to amino acid residues 183 and 184. Consequently, an insert at the *Pst*I site should result in the production of a fused gene product. To effect this insertion, use was made of the homopolymer tailing procedure (Fig. 7.6). The advantage of this method is that in each recombinant molecule the lengths of the repeating G-C base paired joints may be different and at least some of them will be in the correct reading frame.

There is an additional advantage in cloning at the *Pst*I site of pBR322. β-lactamase, the product of the Ap^R gene of pBR322, is a periplasmic

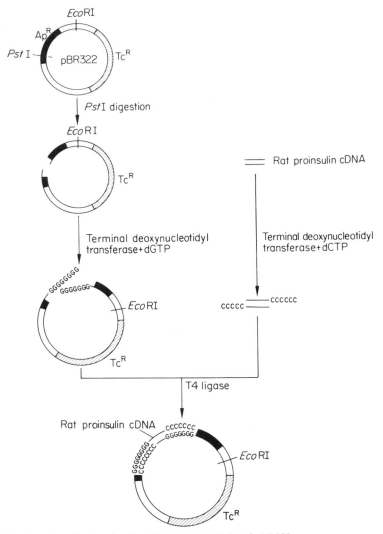

Fig. 7.6   Insertion of rat proinsulin cDNA at the *Pst*I site of pBR322.

protein. It is synthesized as a pre-protein with a 23 amino acid leader sequence which presumably serves as a signal to direct the secretion of the protein to the periplasmic space. This leader is removed as the protein traverses the membrane. Insertion of the structural information for rat proinsulin into the Ap^R gene should cause expression of the insulin sequence as a fusion product transported outside the cell.

Using the hybrid arrested translation procedure (page 70), Villa-Komaroff *et al.* (1978) identified 48 clones containing the insulin sequence. Most of these clones were ampicillin-resistant and hence the active site of

β-lactamase must be between amino acids 23 and 183. The degree of resistance was variable suggesting the expression of different sequences from the inserts in the form of fused translation products, probably differing in length and stability. All 48 clones were screened for the presence of insulin antigenic determinants using an extremely sensitive radioimmunoassay. One clone gave a positive response indicating the presence of a β-lactamase-insulin hybrid polypeptide. Furthermore, in this clone the antigen was detected in the periplasmic space indicating that the fused polypeptide is transported across the membrane as predicted.

Plasmid DNA was isolated from the insulin-secreting clone and the sequences around the oligo (dG.dC) joints determined (Fig. 7.7). Sequencing showed that the insulin region is read in phase; a stretch of six glycine residues connects the alanine at position 182 of β-lactamase to the fourth amino acid, glutamine, of rat proinsulin. In another clone which was examined, the insert was in the correct orientation but was not in phase.

Theoretically it should be possible to use either an oligo (dC.dG) or an oligo (dA.dT) joint and it should not matter which of these four bases is used to tail the *Pst*I cleaved pBR322. In practice, such variations may not work although there is no obvious reason why this should be so. There is, however, precedent for adding oligo dG tails to the *Pst*I cleaved vector. As reference to Fig. 7.7 will show, this procedure results in the re-creation of a *Pst*I substrate site. These considerations apart, cloning in the *Pst*I site with the aid of oligo (dG.dC) tails does appear to be a general method for obtaining gene expression for it has been used by others. For example, expression in *E. coli* has been obtained with DNA sequences coding for mouse dihydrofolate reductase (Chang *et al.* 1978) and Hepatitis B virus antigen (Burrell *et al.* 1979).

The Effect on Protein Production of Gene-promoter Separation

So far, we have described methods for placing a cloned DNA fragment under the control of an *E. coli* promoter. These methods result in the production of a hybrid protein carrying amino-terminal amino acids from either β-lactamase or β-galactosidase. It would, however, be more satisfactory if the gene-promoter fusion produced a native protein. This could be achieved by deleting the translational start signal associated with the promoter and making use only of the one associated with the cloned gene. Of course, it would be essential that the promoter associated S-D sequence be retained.

Cleavage of λ*plac* 5.1 DNA with a combination of *Eco*RI and *Alu*I restriction endonucleases produces a mixture of fragments one of which is 95 base pairs long and retains the *lac* promoter and S-D sequence. Roberts *et al.* (1979) have constructed a series of recombinant plasmids in which this promoter-bearing fragment was located at varying distances in front of

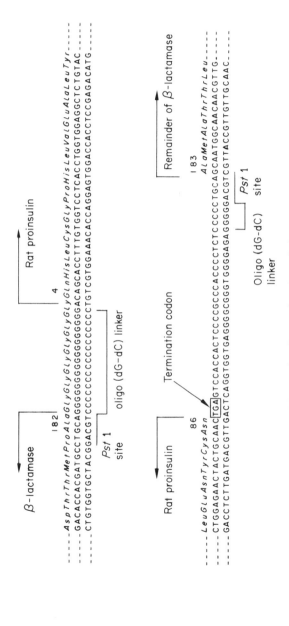

Fig. 7.7 Partial DNA sequence of the plasmid isolated from an insulin secreting clone. Only the sequences around the oligo (dC.dG) joint are shown. It should be noted that the restriction site for *PstI* is -CTGCAG- and that addition of oligo (dC.dG) linkers recreates the *PstI* sites.
-GACGTC-

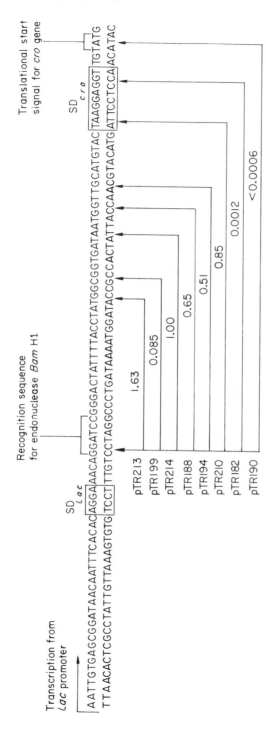

Fig. 7.8 Effect on *cro* protein production of gene-promoter separation. Shown is a portion of the sequence of pTR161 extending from the *lac* promoter to the start-point of translation of the *cro* gene. Also shown is the extent of the deletion in eight derivatives of pTR161. The figures on the brackets indicate the amount of *cro* protein synthesized relative to pTR161. The deletions were created after *Bam* HI digestion by the method outlined in Fig. 7.9.

the λ *cro* gene. Nine different recombinant plasmids were selected, transformed into *E. coli* and the level of *cro* protein in each clone measured. The DNA sequence across the *lac-cro* fusion was also determined in each case. The results obtained are summarized in Fig. 7.8. The most striking feature of these results is the enormous difference (>2000-fold) in the levels of *cro* protein produced by the different recombinants. Since the same promoter is being used in each plasmid it is reasonable to assume that transcription across the *cro* gene is uniform in each case. Thus the differences in protein production must be due to differences in some post-transcriptional process. The *cro* mRNAs transcribed from the various plasmids differ in their leader regions and these differences might affect mRNA stability or processing or ribosome binding efficiency. Whatever the explanation it must account for

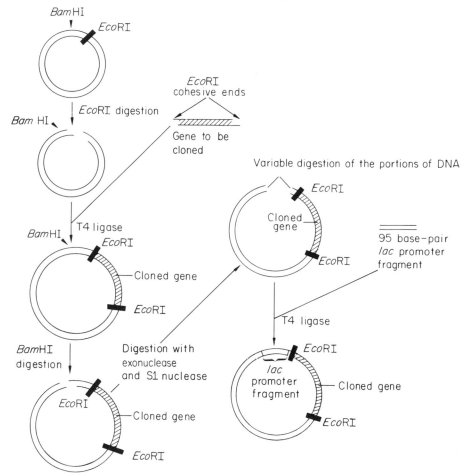

Fig. 7.9 General method for varying the distance between the *lac* promoter and a cloned gene. The example shown uses a hypothetical plasmid carrying unique closely-spaced sites for *Eco* RI and *Bam* HI.

the fact that the deletion in pTR199 is only three bases longer than that in pTR213 and six bases shorter than that in pTR214 yet strains transformed with pTR199 produce less than one tenth the *cro* protein of either of the other two.

The above result suggests a new strategy for maximizing gene expression: namely, a bank of clones is established in which the gene under study is placed at varying distances from the *lac* promoter. These recombinant clones are then screened and the one giving the highest yield selected. Roberts *et al.* (1979) have also described a general method whereby this might be achieved (Fig. 7.9). The gene under study is cloned in a plasmid such that a unique restriction site is located within 100 base pairs of the 5′ end of the gene. The plasmid is opened at that site and varying amounts of DNA excised with exonuclease III and S1 nuclease. The 95 base pair *lac* promoter fragment is then inserted and the plasmid closed by T4 DNA ligase. This produces a set of plasmids bearing the promoter separated by varying distances from the cloned gene.

Stability of Foreign Proteins in *E. coli*
There is currently little information about the stability of proteins in foreign genetic backgrounds. When a cloned gene is not expressed the difficulty is usually ascribed to lack of transcription or translation, and when the cloned gene is expressed it is assumed there is no problem. However, the fact that a cloned gene is expressed in its new host does not necessarily mean that its gene product is stable. Thus, the observation that genes from *Neurospora* and yeast are expressed in *E. coli* only allows us to deduce that the cell contains sufficient of the cloned gene produce to complement its metabolic defect.

There is one documented example of the instability of a cloned-gene product—the degradation of somatostatin in *E. coli* (page 37). In this particular case, degradation was prevented by producing a fused protein consisting of somatostatin and β-galactosidase and subsequently cleaving off the somatostatin with cyanogen bromide. This technique is of limited use for it can only be used when the desired protein contains no methionine. Some of the methods, outlined above, for maximizing gene expression result in the production of fused gene products. It remains to be seen whether such hybrid proteins are inherently more stable.

Detecting Expression of Cloned Genes
When it is known that a cloned DNA fragment codes for a particular protein or RNA species then suitable tests can be devised to determine if that gene is expressed in its new host. Thus, somatostatin or insulin can be detected by sensitive radioimmunoassays, 5S RNA by hybridization to suitable probes and enzymes either by appropriate assay procedures or by complementation of auxotrophic mutations in a suitable host (see page 63).

But how does one detect expression of cloned genes when the function of these genes is not known? The answer is to look for the synthesis of novel proteins or RNA species in cells carrying the recombinant molecules. However, with wild-type cells the detection of new proteins or RNA species is almost impossible because of the concurrent expression of the host genome. Two approaches have been devised to circumvent this problem: expression of plasmid-borne genes can be detected by use of *mini-cells* and λ-borne genes by UV irradiation of the host cell.

Mini-cells are small, spherical, anucleate cells which are produced continuously during the growth of certain mutant strains of bacteria. Because of their size difference, mini-cells and normal-sized cells can be separated easily on sucrose gradients. Mini-cells purified in this way from plasmid-free parents can be shown to contain normal amounts of protein and RNA but to lack DNA. *In vivo,* these mini-cells do not incorporate radioactive precursors into RNA or protein.   By contrast, mini-cells produced from plasmid-carrying parents contain significant amounts of plasmid DNA.   Plasmid-containing mini-cells are capable of RNA and protein synthesis and would appear to be ideal for detecting the expression of genes carried by recombinant plasmids.

In general, there is a correlation between the genotype of a plasmid and the polypeptides synthesized by mini-cells containing that plasmid. However, there are complications since the introduction of deletions or DNA insertions into plasmids can have unpredictable results. For example, a 1 megadalton deletion in a ColE1-derived plasmid prevented the synthesis in mini-cells of polypeptides of 56 000, 42 000, 30 000 and 28 000 daltons. The explanation of this result was apparent after the demonstration that the latter three polypeptides were degradation products of colicin E1 (Meagher *et al.* 1977). The insertion into a kanamycin-resistance gene of a DNA fragment containing the *Eco*RI methylase gene caused the synthesis in mini-cells of *Eco* RI methylase and two other polypeptides. Again, this result could be explained since it was known that the kanamycin-resistance protein was inactivated by the insertion and that there was a portion of another gene on the inserted DNA fragment.   These facts permit the prediction that two new polypeptides would be produced. When the DNA insertion is of unknown function, e.g. randomly-cleaved eukaryotic DNA sequences, interpretation of the expression of the DNA fragments in mini-cells could still be complicated.

The expression of genes cloned in λ vectors can be studied by infection of bacteria previously irradiated so severely with UV light that their own gene expression is effectively eliminated by DNA damage. Under these conditions the products of the cloned genes are seen against a background of λ-specified proteins. If the expression of the DNA insert is independent of λ promoters then even this background can be eliminated by infecting UV-irradiated cells lysogenized with a non-inducible mutant of λ (Newman *et al.* 1979). Under these conditions sufficient λ repressor is present in the cells to prevent transcription of phage genes.

Problems with Gene Expression in Hosts other than *E. coli*

So far our discussion has centred on the problems associated with expression of foreign genes cloned in *E. coli.* However, it is sometimes desirable to clone genes in other prokaryotes, or even to clone prokaryotic genes in eukaryotes. Problems in gene expression undoubtedly will be encountered when cloning in alternative hosts to *E. coli* but as yet there have been too few such experiments to appreciate their frequency. *Bacillus subtilis* can be used as a host for DNA cloning (see page 40) and genes from taxonomically distant organisms can therefore be introduced into this bacterium and their behaviour examined. Unlike genes from *Staphylococcus aureus,* none of several *E. coli* genes tested was found to be expressed in *B. subtilis.* The lack of expression was not due to alterations of the *E. coli* genes since they could be isolated from the *B. subtilis* host and were still functional when reintroduced into *E. coli.* What, then, are the possible barriers to the expression of *E. coli* genes in *B. subtilis*?

The first step in gene expression is the transcription of DNA by RNA polymerase. A comparison of the RNA polymerases from the two organisms has not revealed gross differences but the template specificity of the two polymerases differs in a very interesting way. The *E. coli* enzyme can transcribe equally well DNAs of *E. coli* bacteriophage T4 and of *B. subtilis* bacteriophage φe. By contrast, the *B. subtilis* polymerase is much less active with the *E. coli* than with the *B. subtilis* phage DNAs (Shorenstein & Losick 1973). This behaviour is consistent with the observation that *B. subtilis* genes can function in *E. coli* but the *E. coli* genes cannot function in *B. subtilis.* An indication that different promoter sequences might be recognized by the two enzymes has been obtained by electron microscopy of RNA polymerase-DNA complexes formed *in vitro.* The RNA polymerases from *B. subtilis* and *E. coli* did not bind to the same sites on a recombinant plasmid DNA(pHV14, see page 43) which could function in the two bacterial hosts (Ehrlich *et al.* 1978).

The translational apparatus of *E. coli* and various *Bacillus* spp. are considered to be essentially similar. Nevertheless, intriguing differences have been reported. *E. coli* ribosomes were found to support protein synthesis when directed by four out of five RNAs from Gram-negative cells and with six out of six mRNAs from Gram-positive cells. By contrast, *B. subtilis* ribosomes were not active with any of the mRNAs from Gram-negative bacteria nor three out of four mRNAs from Gram-positive bacteria (Stallcup *et al.* 1974). Clearly, barriers to heterospecific gene expression also exist at the level of translation.

If differences exist in the gene-to-phenotype biochemical pathways of Gram-negative and Gram-positive bacteria then it would hardly be surprising if there were significant differences in the same pathways between prokaryotic and eukaryotic cells. The ability to construct plasmid vectors which function in both *E. coli* and yeast (see page 44) should provide a useful method for analysing such differences and devising means to combat the problems they will create in cloning prokaryotic genes in eukaryotes.

Chapter 8. Cloning in Mammalian Cells

From the preceding chapters it should be apparent that there is a wide range of both plasmid and phage vectors available for cloning in prokaryotic cells, particularly *E. coli*. This is in marked contrast to the situation with mammalian cells where the only vectors which have been developed are derived from simian virus 40 (SV40). SV40 is a papovavirus and there are a number of other papovaviruses with different host ranges eg. polyoma virus, which could be developed in a similar way.

SV40 is particularly attractive as a vector for a number of reasons. These are:

(1) The genome consists of a single, small, covalently-closed circular DNA molecule whose entire nucleotide sequence has been determined (Fiers *et al.* 1978, Reddy *et al.* 1978);

(2) The viral DNA is obtainable in large quantities;

(3) The genomic regions responsible for the various viral functions have been accurately located with respect to a detailed physical map of the DNA (Fiers *et al.* 1978; Reddy *et al.* 1978);

(4) The viral genome can multiply vegetatively or as an integral part of cellular chromosomes;

(5) A wealth of information exists on the replication and expression of the viral genome.

Sufficient information about the biology of SV40 is presented below to enable the reader to appreciate its potential as a vector. For a more detailed analysis of the biology of the virus, particularly the events leading to transformation of cells in culture, the reader should consult an advanced virology treatise (e.g. Luria *et al.* 1978) and the papers of Fiers *et al.* (1978) and Reddy *et al.* (1978).

Basic Properties of SV40

The virus particle has a mol. wt. of 28 megadaltons and contains a circular double-stranded DNA molecule of mol. wt. 3 megadaltons. Bound to the viral DNA are four of the five main host histones, H4, H2a, H2b and H3 with H1 being absent. The capsid is constructed from 420 sub-units of the 47 000 dalton mol. wt. polypeptide VP1. Two minor polypeptides, VP2 and VP3, which consist largely of identical amino acid sequences, are also present.

When SV40 virus enters a susceptible monkey cell it generally disappears without a trace. Only about 1% of the infecting particles multiply in a conventional lytic cycle culminating in the production of new virus particles. When SV40 infects a mouse or hamster cell no progeny are made but approximately 10^{-5} infected cells become transformed. Cells in which a papovavirus multiplies are called *permissive* and cells in which viral growth does not occur are *non-permissive*. Generally speaking, a permissive cell line is derived from an animal in which a given virus normally reproduces. Non-permissive cell lines usually originate from animals which are insusceptible to the virus. Thus, SV40 multiplies in monkey cells but never mouse cells, although it can transform the latter. Highly purified DNA of SV40 is infectious and infection of permissive cells leads to a lytic response and of non-permissive cells to a transforming response.

The lytic infection of monkey cells by SV40 can be divided into three distinct phases. During the first eight hours the virus particles are uncoated and the DNA moves to the host cell nucleus. In the following four hours, the *early* phase, synthesis of early mRNA and early protein occur and there is a virus-induced stimulation of host cell DNA synthesis. The *late* phase occupies the next thirty six hours and during this period there is synthesis of viral DNA, late mRNA and late protein and culminates in virus assembly and cellular disintegration. A point worth noting is that early and late mRNAs are transcribed from different strands of DNA (the r and 1 strands respectively—Fig. 8.1).

In recent years a large number of different temperature-sensitive (*ts*)

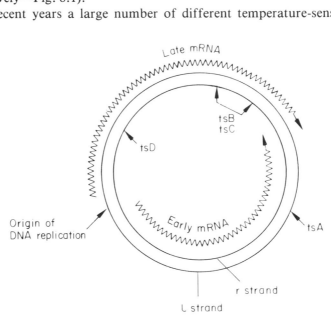

Fig. 8.1 Locations of the four groups of temperature sensitive mutants of SV40. The B & C mutants appear to be in the same gene.

mutants have been isolated in SV40 after treatment with nitrous acid (Yang Chou & Martin 1974). These mutants fall into four complementation groups (Fig. 8.1). Three of these complementation groups correspond to the late genes coding for structural proteins and the fourth to a gene which codes for the earliest protein made in infected cells, the T antigen. The T antigen is the product of the A gene and may play a critical role in cellular transformation. The major physiological consequence of infecting monkey cells at the non-permissive temperature with a tsA mutant of SV40 is a block in the initiation of viral DNA synthesis. Impairment of the induction of cellular DNA synthesis may also occur.

RNA species which code for the SV40 structural proteins begin to accumulate at the same time as DNA replication starts. It should be noted that these late mRNAs are transcribed from a different DNA strand to the early mRNA (Fig. 8.1). Many of the SV40 particles infecting non-permissive cells (e.g. mouse 3T3 cells) go through the early stage of reproduction. Early SV40 mRNA is made, as is the T antigen and some SV40 DNA. However, no viral structural proteins are synthesized even though much late SV40 mRNA is detected, especially in the nucleus.

Restriction Map of SV40 DNA

Before considering the use of SV40 as a vector, it is necessary to have a restriction map of the viral DNA. Such a map is shown in Fig. 8.2. For convenience the different restriction sites are assigned map co-ordinates between 0 and 1 with the *Eco* RI site arbitrarily assigned position 0/1. The origin of replication, *ori* is located at co-ordinate 0.67.

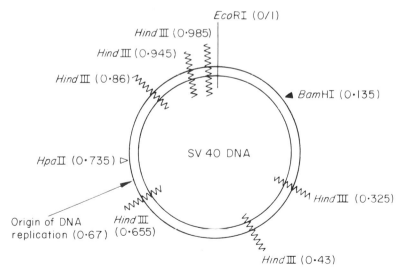

Fig. 8.2 Restriction endonuclease sites on SV40 DNA. The map co-ordinates of each site are shown in parentheses.

SV40 as a Vector

Wild-type SV40 cannot be used as a vector since the addition of exogenous DNA would generate a DNA molecule too large to be packaged into viral particles. However, SV40 mutants lacking the entire late region can be propagated in mixed infections with a helper virus, e.g. a tsA mutant, that can provide the missing function (Mertz & Berg 1974). Based on this observation Goff & Berg (1976) prepared an SV40 vector by excising virtually the entire late region of the viral DNA by cleavage with *Hpa* II and *Bam* HI restriction endonucleases (Fig. 8.3). Cleavage with these two enzymes produces fragments approximately 0.6 and 0.4 of the genome length. These two fragments were separated by electrophoresis and the smaller fragment discarded. The large fragment, called SVGT-1, was then modified by the addition of 5′ poly (dA) tails using deoxynucleotidyl terminal transferase.

A suitable insert was prepared by cleaving λDNA with *Eco* RI and *Hind* III restriction endonucleases. This treatment yielded 12 DNA fragments which were separated by electrophoresis in agarose. Fragment 8 is 1.48 Kb in length and contains *ori,* the origin of λ DNA replication, two structural genes, cII and *cro,* as well as four transcriptional promoters. After elution of fragment 8 from the agarose gel it was modified by the addition of poly (dT) tails (Fig. 8.3). SVGT-1 containing the poly (dA) termini and the poly (dT) tailed fragment 8 were mixed and annealed. The annealed DNA was then used to infect monkey kidney cells in the presence or absence of tsA helper virus DNA. At the restrictive temperature (41°C) tsA DNA alone gave no plaques, the annealed DNA alone gave no plaques, but infection with the two DNAs together produced 2.5×10^3 pfu/μg of annealed DNA.

Thirty four plaques from the mixedly infected cultures were extracted, mixed with more tsA mutant virus and used to infect fresh monkey cells at 41°C. DNA was extracted from the progeny virus and the presence of the λ phage DNA segment was detected by measuring the reassociation kinetics with ^{3}H-labelled λ fragment 8 DNA. DNA from infections with 9 of the 34 plaques caused a striking increase in the reassociation rate of the labelled λ DNA fragment indicating the presence of high levels of the λ-SVGT hybrid. Heteroduplex analysis and restriction endonuclease mapping of the viral DNA from these 9 infected cultures confirmed that it was the expected mixture of tsA DNA and recombinant DNA.

Although the SVGT-λ hybrid DNA replicated in monkey cells in the presence of tsA helper DNA, the λ DNA sequences were not transcribed. At a time after infection when substantial amounts of SV40-specific RNA could be detected no λ-specific RNA was found. The search for new polypeptides in the λ-SVGT hybrid infected cells was also fruitless. These disappointingly negative results were still obtained when hybrids with the λ insert in opposite orientations were used.

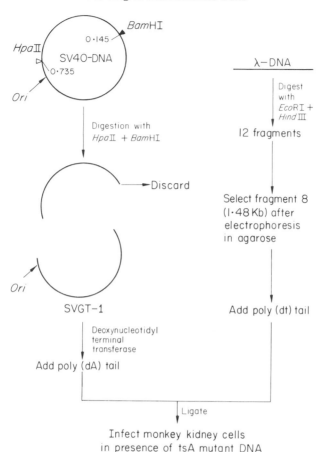

Fig. 8.3 Construction of an SV40-λ DNA hybrid as described in the text. The bold lines represent duplex DNA molecules.

Hamer (1977) synthesized SV40-*E. coli* Su⁺III recombinant DNA by a method similar to that of Goff & Berg (1976). In contrast to the results of the latter workers, Hamer (1977) found that monkey cells infected with the Sv40-Su⁺III recombinant DNA synthesized surprisingly large amounts of RNA complementary to the insert. The normal product of the *E. coli* Su⁺III gene is a suppressor RNA but all attempts to isolate a free or charged tRNA were unsuccessful.

The failure of both Goff & Berg (1976) and Hamer (1977) to get faithful transcription of their DNA inserts could simply be due to a failure of monkey cells to recognize prokaryotic promoters. A more likely explanation, however, is provided by analyses of transcription of SV40 DNA.

Transcription of SV40 DNA

The transcription of the three late SV40 genes is a complex process. There are two reasons for this. Firstly, the three genes overlap (Fig. 8.4) with the gene for VP3 being entirely contained within the gene for VP2. Secondly, and more importantly, the late mRNAs are composite structures produced by splicing together nucleotide sequences transcribed from non-adjacent DNA segments. Only two late mRNAs are produced, a 19S RNA species coding for proteins VP2 and VP3 and a 16S species coding for protein VP1. Both species comprise a *leader sequence,* including a 5′ terminal cap, which is involved in translational control and an RNA *body,* including a 3′ poly-A tail, containing the nucleotide sequence to be translated. For both late mRNA species the leader sequence is transcribed from the 1 strand between map co-ordinates 0.69 and 0.76. The body of 19S mRNA is transcribed from the 1 strand between co-ordinates 0.77 and 0.175, whereas the body of the 16S RNA is transcribed from the 1 strand between co-ordinates 0.94 and 0.175 (Fig. 8.4). Thus, both the 16S and 19S mRNAs contain the sequence coding for VP1 but this is a translation product only of the 16S mRNA.

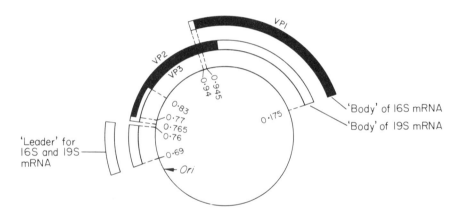

Fig. 8.4   The composite structure of SV40 late mRNAs. The map of SV40 DNA is shown on the inner circle. The regions coding for the structure of VP1, VP2 and VP3 are shown as shaded regions within the 'bodies' of the 19S and 16S mRNAs. Note that the coding region for VP3 lies entirely inside that of VP2 and overlaps that of VP1. Note also that the 'body' of the 19S mRNA is much larger than the region coding for VP2 and VP3.

Deletion mutants have been obtained which lack the 3′ boundary of the late region leader segments. RNA transcribed from these mutants is not processed into mature 16 or 19S mRNA, presumably because splicing cannot occur. The SV40 vectors described earlier resemble these deletion mutants in that they had lost some or all of the sequences required for splicing. Thus the failure to obtain discrete mRNAs with the first SV40 recombinant molecules probably stems from the disruption of post-transcriptional splicing reactions.

Construction of an Improved SV40 Vector

From the information presented above on transcription of SV40 it is clear that the ideal vector would retain all the regions implicated in transcriptional initiation and termination, splicing and polyadenylation. Inspection of the SV40 restriction map (Fig. 8.2) reveals two restriction-endonuclease sites that could be used to generate a suitable vector. Firstly, there is a *Hind* III site at the map position 0.945 which is 6 nucleotides *proximal* to the initiation codon for VP1 (Fig. 8.5) and 50 nucleotides *distal* to the site at which the leader sequence is joined to the body of 16S mRNA. Secondly, the *Bam* HI site at map position 0.145 is 50 nucleotides proximal to the termination codon for VP1 translation and 150 nucleotides before the poly A sequence at the 3′ end of 16S RNA (Fig. 8.5). If the DNA between co-ordinates 0.945 and 0.145 were removed the remaining molecule could be used as a vector for it would retain:

(a) The origin of replication;
(b) The regions at which splicing and polyadenylation occur;
(c) The entire early region and hence could be complemented by a tsA mutant.

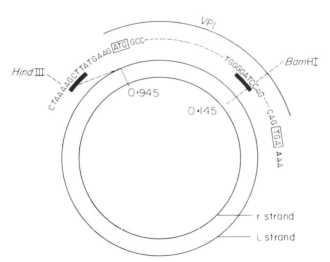

Fig. 8.5 Location of the *Hind* III and *Bam* HI cleavage sites in relation to the coding sequence for VP1. The triplets enclosed in boxes show the initiation and termination signals for translation of VP1. The sequences underlined are the recognition sites for the *Hind* III and *Bam* HI restriction endonucleases.

Such a vector (SVGT-5) has now been constructed and used successfully to clone the rabbit β-globin gene in monkey kidney cells (Mulligan *et al.* 1979).

The first step in constructing SVGT-5 was to digest partially SV40 DNA with restriction endonuclease *Hind* III. The digestion products were separated by electrophoresis and full-length molecules, i.e. those with a single cut, selected. Clearly these full-length molecules could have a cut at any one of the six *Hind* III sites on SV40 DNA. The mixture of different full-length molecules was then digested with a mixture of restriction endonucleases *Bam* HI and *Eco* RI and fragments of 4.2 Kb (SVGT-5) selected by electrophoresis on an agarose gel. Examination of the SV40 restriction map (Fig. 8.6) shows that cleavage of the *Hind* III site at position 0.945 and at the *Bam* HI site produces the desired SVGT-5 fragment which is 4.2 Kb long. However, cleavage at the *Hind* III site at position 0.325 and at the *Bam* HI site would produce a fragment of similar size. Since only the latter fragment contains an *Eco* RI site it can be selectively eliminated by including endonuclease *Eco* RI in the digestion mixture.

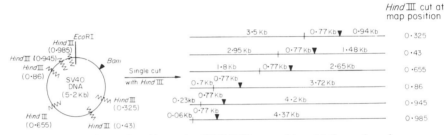

Fig. 8.6 Molecules produced by cutting SV40 DNA once with restriction endonuclease *Hind* III. Note that when these six different molecules are cleaved with a mixture of *Eco* RI and *Bam* HI restriction endonucleases only one of them will produce a fragment 4.2 Kb in length. For convenience only one strand of the DNA is shown.

Example of the Use of SVGT-5: Cloning of the Rabbit β-Globin Gene in Monkey Kidney Cells

The starting point for this experiment was the recombinant plasmid pβG1 which contains the rabbit β-globin coding sequence. pβG1 was constructed by Maniatis *et al.* (1976) by inserting a cDNA copy of purified rabbit β-globin mRNA at the *Eco* RI site of plasmid pMB9 using the homopolymer tailing method. Nucleotide sequence analysis confirmed that pβG1 contained the entire β-globin coding sequence, all of the 3′ and 80% of the 5′ non-coding sequences in β-globin mRNA (Efstratiadis *et al.* 1976). Basically, the experiment was conducted in two stages:

(a) excision of the β-globin cDNA from pβG1 and its modification to produce *Hind* III cohesive sites at either end;
(b) insertion of the altered cDNA into SVGT-5.

Alteration of β-globin cDNA (Fig. 8.7)

pβG1 was incubated at 50°C in the presence of S1 nuclease. At this temperature the poly (dA.dT) joints melt and the resulting single-strands are digested with nuclease S1. The two fragments were separated by electro-

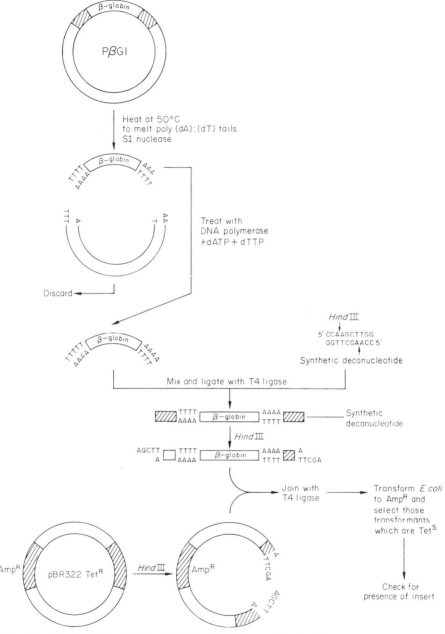

Fig. 8.7   Cloning of the β-globin cDNA in pBR322 (see text for details).

phoresis and the β-globin cDNA fragment isolated and treated with DNA polymerase I to convert the 'ragged' single-stranded ends to 'blunt' ends. A synthetic decanucleotide was then attached to either end of the cDNA

Future Prospects

The above experiments clearly show that a foreign gene can be expressed in
monkey cells during lytic infection with a recombinant SV40 genome.
However, ideally we require gene expression in the absence of cell lysis.
SVGT-5-RaβG should be able to transform a variety of non-permissive
mammalian cells, e.g. rat, mouse and human cells. Since integrated SV40
genomes do not express late genes, transformed cells are not likely to
make β-globin or any other protein whose coding sequence is cloned in
SVGT-5. Thus, there is a need for SV40 vectors in which transcription of
the exogenous gene is under early control and undoubtedly the isolation of
such vectors will be reported in the near future.

Co-transformation of Mammalian Cells [†]

Just as with prokaryotes, specific genes or entire viral genomes can be
introduced into cultured mammalian cells by DNA-mediated gene transfer.
Indeed, the ability to transfect cells was an essential prerequisite for the
development of SV40-derived vectors described above. However, the
transformation procedures currently in use are highly inefficient and the
isolation of cells transformed with genes which do not code for selectable
markers is problematic. It will be recalled that when cloning in prokaryotes
with plasmid vectors it is usual to use a vector with a readily scorable
phenotype in order to select those rare cells which have been transformed.
Wigler *et al.* (1979) have now devised a somewhat analogous procedure for
use with mammalian cells which involves co-transformation of cells with
two *physically-unlinked* sets of genes. The rationale of this procedure is as
follows. Studies of transformation of bacteria have shown that a small but
selectable sub-population of cells is competent in transformation. If this
were also true for animal cells then biochemical transformants would
represent a sub-population of competent cells which could integrate other
unlinked genes at frequencies higher than the general population. Specific
details of the method are outlined below.

Whereas wild-type mouse cells can grow in a medium containing
hypoxanthine, aminopterin and thymine (HAT medium), mutant cells
lacking thymidine kinase (tk⁻ cells) are unable to do so. It is relatively easy
to purify the thymidine kinase gene from herpes simplex virus and the
addition of this gene to tk⁻ cells results in the appearance of stable transformants expressing the viral gene. Such transformants can be selected by
their ability to grow in HAT medium. To obtain co-transformants, cultures
are exposed to the thymidine kinase gene in the presence of a vast excess of
a well-defined DNA sequence for which hybridization probes are available.
Tk⁺ transformants are isolated and scored by molecular hybridization for

[†] In this section 'transformation' refers to 'genetic transformation', analogous to bacterial
transformation, and NOT to cellular transformation.

the co-transfer of additional DNA sequences.

Wigler *et al.* (1979) demonstrated the co-transformation of mouse tk⁻ cells with pBR322, bacteriophage φX174 DNA and rabbit β-globin gene sequences and we shall use their φX experiments for illustrative purposes. φX replicative form DNA was cleaved with *Pst* I which recognizes a single site in the circular genome. 500 pg of the purified thymidine kinase gene were mixed with 10 μg of *Pst* I cleaved φX replicative form DNA. This DNA mixture was added to tk⁻ mouse cells and 25 tk⁺ transformants were observed per 10^6 cells after 2 weeks in HAT medium. To determine if these tk⁺ transformants also contained φX DNA sequences, high mol. wt. DNA from the transformants was cleaved with *Eco* RI which recognizes no sites in the φX genome. The cleaved DNA was fractionated by agarose gel electrophoresis, transferred to nitrocellulose filters by 'Southern blotting' and annealed with labelled φX DNA. These annealing experiments demonstrated that 14 out of 16 tk⁺ transformants had acquired one or more φX sequences.

Are φX Sequences Integrated into Cellular DNA?

Cleavage of DNA from φX transformants with *Eco* RI generates a series of fragments which contain φX sequences. These fragments could reflect integration events or, alternatively, tandem arrays of complete or partial φX sequences which are not integrated into cellular DNA. To distinguish between these possibilities, transformed cell DNA was cut with either *Bam* HI or *Eco* RI, neither of which cleaves the φX genome. If the φX DNA sequences were not integrated, neither of these enzymes would cleave the φX fragments. Identical patterns would be generated from undigested DNA and from DNA cleaved with either of these enzymes. If the sequences were integrated, then the two restriction endonucleases would generate different patterns of fragments since they recognize different sites on the DNA.

When DNA from a number of φX-containing tk⁺ clones was cleaved with *Bam* HI or *Eco* RI and analysed by Southern blotting, the annealing pattern with *Eco* RI fragments differed from that observed with the *Bam* generated fragments. By contrast, the profile obtained with undigested DNA revealed annealing only in very high mol. wt. regions. These data showed that most, if not all, of the φX sequences were integrated into cellular DNA. Furthermore, when the location of the φX sequences in transformed cells was determined by sub-cellular fractionation it was clear that the majority of them were in high mol. wt. nuclear DNA.

How Much of the φX Genome is Present in Transformed Cells?

The annealing profiles of DNA from transformed clones digested with enzymes that do not cleave the φX genome provide evidence that integration of φX sequences has occurred. By contrast, annealing profiles of DNA from transformed clones digested with enzymes which cleave within the ϕX genome allow the determination of what proportion of the genome is present and how these sequences are arranged following integration. Cleavage of ϕX DNA with *Hpa* I generates three fragments—two 'internal' fragments of 3.7 Kb and 1.3 Kb and one 'bridge' fragment of 0.5 Kb which spans the *Pst* I site which is cleaved prior to co-transformation. The annealing profile observed by Southern blotting of *Hpa* I-digested DNA from a ϕX-containing tk$^+$ clone showed the presence of the two 'internal' fragments. When the experiment was repeated with a number of other restriction endonucleases it became clear that whereas the 'internal' fragments were always present, the 'bridge' fragments spanning the *Pst* I cleavage site were reduced or absent.

The above results give some indication of the process whereby integration took place. If either precise circularization or the formation of linear concatemers had occurred at the *Pst* I cleavage site, and if integration occurred at random points along this DNA, then the cleavage maps of transformed cell DNA would resemble the cleavage maps of ϕX DNA. Since the 'bridge' fragment was present in reduced amounts, if at all, the ϕX DNA must have integrated as a linear molecule.

Implications of Co-transformation
Theoretically, the co-transformation system described above should allow the introduction and stable integration into cultured cells of virtually any defined gene without recourse to viral vectors. Therefore, has cloning in eukaryotes been rendered redundant? The answer is no. Firstly, the usefulness of the co-transformation method will depend to a large extent on its generality, i.e. can it be used with cell lines other than tk$^-$ mutants? Secondly, successful co-transformation with a particular gene requires that the gene be purified, or at least greatly enriched, and that a suitable probe is available for its detection. From the results described in previous chapters it is clear that in most instances the easiest way to purify a gene is to clone it. Nevertheless, co-transformation of mammalian cells is an important technique and the results reported so far raise all sorts of intriguing questions, e.g. what is the exact mechanism whereby foreign DNA is integrated into mammalian cells?

The early experiments on uptake of foreign DNA by plant cells, as carried out by Ledoux and his colleagues, were described in Chapter 1. Because of the insensitivity of the methods used to detect DNA incorporation these experiments were not conclusive. It will be recalled that we pointed out that more recently developed techniques such as 'Southern blotting' would provide positive proof of foreign DNA integration if it had occurred. The experiments of Wigler *et al.* (1979) described above, as well as the experiments on yeast transformation described earlier (page 45) demonstrate the usefulness of 'Southern blotting' in this respect.

Chapter 9. Possible Vectors for Cloning DNA in Plant Cells

Cloning of exogenous DNA in prokaryotic cells is so simple that it is now routinely performed in hundreds of laboratories around the world. Cloning in eukaryotes is at a much more primitive state principally because of the lack of suitable vectors. At the present moment the only vector available for eukaryotic cells is SV40 whose subjugation was described in the previous chapter. Although no vectors are currently available for use with higher plants there are two possible candidates—the DNA plant viruses and the Ti plasmid of *Agrobacterium tumefaciens*. The aim of this chapter is to provide readers with sufficient background information to enable them to follow the developments which will surely take place in this field in the next 5 years.

DNA PLANT VIRUSES

There are two groups of plant viruses which contain DNA—the Caulimoviruses, which have double-stranded DNA, and the Geminiviruses, which have single-stranded DNA. Since most of the technology of gene manipulation involves double-stranded DNA the Caulimoviruses are of most interest and are the only ones considered here. A detailed review of the literature on Caulimoviruses has been provided by Shepherd (1976).

Biological Properties of Caulimoviruses

Only a small number of Caulimoviruses are known and the commonest are listed in Table 9.1. They all have a similar particle size, *in vivo* behaviour and several are serologically related. Caulimoviruses have restricted host ranges and are confined to a few closely related plants in nature. There appears to be little, if any, overlap between the host ranges of the individual viruses within the group, in spite of some of the close serological affinities. Cauliflower mosaic virus (CaMV), for example, infects only members of the Cruciferae in nature although it is experimentally transmissible to a few plants outside this family. The Caulimoviruses are widely distributed throughout the temperate regions of the world and are responsible for a number of economically important diseases of cultivated crops.

Most of the isolates of Caulimoviruses that have been tested are transmitted by aphids in a non-persistent or stylet-borne manner. Successful transfer

Table 9.1   Host range of some caulimoviruses.

Virus	Host range	Serological relatedness
Carnation etched ring virus (CERV)	Caryophyllaceae	Related to CaMV and DaMV
Cauliflower mosaic virus (CaMV)	Several Cruciferae and two species of Solanaceae	Related to CERV and DaMV
Dahlia mosaic virus (DaMV)	Several Compositae and some Amaranthaceae, Chenopodiaceae and Solanaceae	Related to CaMV and CERV
Mirabilis mosaic virus	*Mirabilis* sp. (Nyataginaceae)	Unrelated to CaMV or DaMV
Strawberry vein banding virus	Fragaria sp. (Rosaceae)	—

of CaMV by aphids requires the presence of a transmission factor in infected cells. This factor is not part of the virus particle but must be synthesized in response to infection since two non-transmissible isolates of CaMV have been identified (Lung & Pirone 1974).

The remainder of our discussion on Caulimoviruses will be restricted to the best-studied example, CaMV. However, it is reasonable to assume that CaMV does not differ significantly from the other Caulimoviruses.

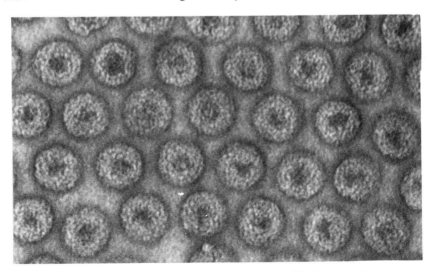

Fig. 9.1   Semi-crystalline array of cauliflower mosaic virus purified from turnip (approx. magnification 200 000). The dark spots in the centres of the particles are typical and are the result of the outer protein shell being sucked into the hollow core during preparation for electron microscopy. (Photograph courtesy of M. Webb, National Vegetable Research Station.)

The Structure of CaMV

CaMV particles are isometric and about 50nm in diameter (Fig. 9.1). There are probably four structural polypeptides but only two of these account for over 90% of the viral protein. The major components have mol. wts. of 37 000 and 64 000 and are present in a molar ratio of 5 to 1. From the proportion of these polypeptide species and the mol. wt. of the virus particle (23 megadaltons) the most likely structure is an outer shell of 420 molecules of the 37 000 species surrounding a core of 60 molecules of the 64 000 species (Hull & Shepherd 1976). The two remaining polypeptides have much higher mol. wts. (96 000 and 88 000) and may be glycoproteins. Their function is not known.

Properties of CaMV DNA

The genome of CaMV consists of a double-stranded circular DNA molecule of mol. wt. 4.5-5 megadaltons (Hull & Shepherd 1977). An unusual feature of CaMV DNA is the presence of single-stranded gaps (Volvovitch *et al.* 1978). These can be demonstrated by electrophoresing in agarose DNA which has been treated with the single-strand specific nuclease S1. The DNA from most isolates of CaMV has three gaps or nicks, two in one strand and one in the other (Fig. 9.2) and in any one strain the positions of the gaps are fixed with respect to restriction endonuclease cleavage sites. The 5' end of the DNA at each gap can be labelled with ^{32}P using poly-nucleotide kinase suggesting that the 5' termini are hydroxyl groups. Nothing is known about the physiological significance of these interruptions nor is

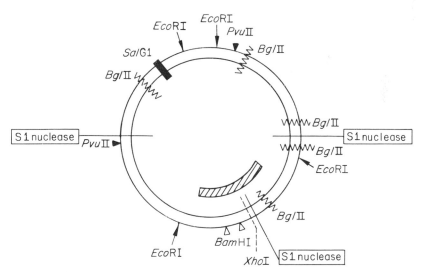

Fig. 9.2 Restriction endonuclease map of the cabbage B-JI strain of CaMV. The hatched bar represents the segment deleted in the CM4-184 isolate. Note that the single-strand gaps (sites of attack by S1 nuclease) are not all in the same strand.

it known for certain if they exist in the virus particle. The gaps could result from the extraction procedure and be a reflection of something else in the intact particle, e.g. covalently bound protein. The identification of a strain of CaMV with only two gaps in its DNA may help to elucidate the function of such single-strand interruptions.

Another unusual feature of CaMV DNA is the presence of a number of short sequences of ribonucleotides in a certain proportion of the population of molecules (Hull & Shepherd 1977). Ribonucleotides have been detected and comprise less than 1% of the total nucleotides. These ribonucleotides could be primers for DNA synthesis which have not been excised during replication.

Restriction Endonuclease Cleavage Sites on CaMV DNA

The genomes of 25 different isolates of CaMV have been mapped using restriction endonucleases (Meagher *et al.* 1977, Hull & Howell 1978). At least seven different groups have been recognized on the basis of *Eco* RI cleavage. Most of these groups differ in the presence or absence of cleavage sites and a detailed map is shown for one isolate only (Fig. 8.1). The differences between maps of the isolates indicate that one region of the genome is subject to considerable change while the rest is more highly conserved. Two isolates have DNA molecules which differ in size from those of the others. Isolate CM4-184 has a deletion of about 0.25 megadaltons (Fig. 9.2) while the 'Australian' isolate appears to have a small addition (0.05 megadaltons). As well as variation in restriction endonuclease digestion patterns between isolates there is often evidence of heterogeneity within an isolate, restriction fragments being produced in less than stoichiometric amounts. The exact reason for these intra-strain variations is not known but may in fact be trivial.

Transcription of CaMV

Relatively little is known about the molecular events occurring in CaMV infected cells since a suitable plant cell culture system, using protoplasts, has only recently been developed. About 2.5 days following synchronous infection a stable RNA species of mol. wt. 1.5-1.8 megadaltons coded by the CaMV genome appeared in infected protoplasts. This RNA species hybridized to only one DNA strand, the strand with only one discontinuity. In addition, this RNA was polyadenylated and was associated with polyribosomes suggesting that it has a messenger function.

Although only a single viral-specified mRNA has been detected in infected cells the transcription pattern of CaMV must be more complex. In the absence of overlapping genes or transcription from both strands the coding potential of CaMV DNA is not sufficient for the four structural polypeptides and the aphid acquisition factor.

The Usefulness of CaMV as a Vector

There are a number of contra-indications for the use of CaMV as a vector. Firstly, Szeto *et al.* (1977) found that whereas purified CaMV DNA was infectious, viral DNA that had been cleaved at the single *Sal* GI site and religated was not. The reason for this is not clear. Perhaps there are two closely spaced *Sal* sites and a fragment, too small to be detected in gels, was lost. Alternatively, CaMV DNA may have some crucial secondary structure that is lost on cleavage. This result was particularly disappointing for it meant that Szeto *et al.* (1977) had no way to test the infectivity of the entire CaMV genome which they had cloned in *E. coli*. Had the cloned molecule been infectious for plants it would have provided valuable information about the dispensability of the single-strand gaps and the ribonucleotides found in native DNA.

A second disadvantage is that CaMV DNA has multiple cleavage sites for most of the commonly used restriction endonucleases and this will limit the usefulness of wild isolates of CaMV. However, given the state of present technology, many of these sites probably could be removed and the CM4-184 variant would be a good starting point. Thirdly, there is no evidence that CaMV integrates into host cell chromosomes. Since neither the virus nor its DNA is seed transmitted how would the recombinant molecule be transmitted from generation to generation? The virus moves systemically through infected hosts and so vegetative propagation might permit the maintenance of the cloned DNA.

Even if the problem of the non-infectivity of CaMV DNA can be overcome we are still a long way away from using CaMV as a vector. Nothing is known about the gene functions nor the minimum amount of DNA necessary for self-replication. Acquisition of similar information about SV40 occurred slowly despite the fact that its study has attracted infinitely more effort than the Caulimoviruses. Add to that the problems of identifying mutants of CaMV in the absence of a suitable plaque assay and the magnitude of the problem becomes apparent.

AGROBACTERIUM TUMEFACIENS AND THE INDUCTION OF CROWN GALL

Crown gall tumours (Fig. 9.3) are induced in a wide variety of dicotyledenous plants by inoculation of wound sites with virulent *Agrobacterium tumefaciens*. The bacteria induce two types of tumour: one class of strains induces tumours with a rough surface whereas the other class induces tumours with a smooth surface and also causes malformed leaf structures. Adventitious roots may form from both types of tumour due to high auxin production.

The plant cells in the tumour acquire a number of new properties. Firstly, they show phytohormone independent growth. Secondly, they have the

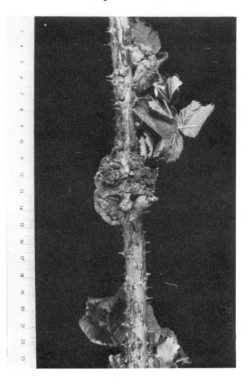

Fig. 9.3   Crown gall on (A) blackberry cane and (B) two-year-old cherry rootstock (courtesy Dr C. M. E. Garrett, East Malling Research Station).

capacity to cause overgrowths when grafted onto healthy plants. Finally, most tumours contain one or other of the unusual guanido amino acids octopine or nopaline. Crown gall tumour cells continue to synthesize octopine or nopaline in tissue culture and some of the plants regenerated from nopaline containing tumour-tissue continue to synthesize nopaline (Schell & Van Montagu 1977).

The ability of the tumour cells to synthesize either octopine or nopaline is a property conferred on the plant cells by the bacteria. Both octopine and nopaline can be used as the sole nitrogen source for growth of *Agrobacterium tumefaciens*. In general, the strains that utilize octopine induce tumours that synthesize octopine, and those that utilize nopaline induce tumours that synthesize nopaline (Bomhoff *et al.* 1976, Montoya *et al.* 1977). However, there are several notable exceptions. Some strains utilize both octopine and nopaline but the tumours induced by these strains produce only nopaline. Others utilize nopaline but the tumours induced synthesize neither octopine nor nopaline. Thus octopine or nopaline biosynthesis is not an essential prerequisite for tumour formation. Mutants have been isolated from a number of either octopine- or nopaline-utilizing strains which were defective in the genes specifying either octopine or nopaline oxidase. These mutants still retained the permease for the octopine and nopaline, were still virulent and the tumours which they induced still synthesized normal amounts of these amino acids (Montoya *et al.* 1977). Clearly the bacterial genes which determine octopine or nopaline biosynthesis by tumour cells are distinct from the genes that determine their catabolism by the bacteria.

The 'Tumour Inducing Principle' and the Ti Plasmid
Ever since Smith & Townsend showed in 1907 that a bacterium is the causative agent of crown gall tumours, the most intriguing question has been, how does the bacterium induce these modifications? Elegant experiments of Braun and his collaborators convincingly showed that the continued presence of viable bacteria is not required for tumour formation (Braun & Stonier 1958). The bacteria do not penetrate into the plant cells that are converted into tumour cells. Rather, bacteria penetrate into the intercellular spaces and into injured cells and only attach themselves to the wall of healthy plant cells. Attention has thus been focused on the identification of a putative 'tumour inducing principle' elaborated by the bacteria and transferred to the plant. There is now considerable evidence that the tumour inducing principle is a fragment of a plasmid.

Zaenen *et al.* (1974) first noted that virulent strains of *A. tumefaciens* harbour large plasmids (95-160 megadaltons) and there is now good evidence that the virulence trait is plasmid borne. Virulence is lost when the bacteria are cured of the plasmid and with some strains this can be achieved by growing the cells at 37°C instead of 28°C. Cured strains also lose the

capacity to utilize octopine or nopaline (Van Larebeke *et al.* 1974, Watson
et al. 1975). Virulence is acquired by avirulent strains when a virulence
plasmid is re-introduced (Bomhoff *et al.* 1976, Gordon *et al.* 1979). If the
plasmid from a nopaline-containing strain is transferred to an avirulent
derivative of a previously octopine utilizing strain, the avirulent strain
acquires the ability to utilize nopaline rather than octopine. Also, the
tumours induced by the ex-conjugant contain nopaline. The virulence
plasmid can also be transferred to the legume symbiont *Rhizobium trifolii*
which becomes oncogenic and acquires the ability to utilize either nopaline
or octopine depending on the donor.

From the above information it is clear that the virulence plasmids
are essential for oncogenicity and for this reason they are referred to
as Ti (tumour-inducing) plasmids. Furthermore, the genetic information
specifying bacterial utilization of octopine and nopaline and their synthesis
by plants must also be plasmid borne.

Plasmids in the octopine group have been shown to be closely related
to each other while those in the nopaline group are considerably more
diverse (Currier & Nester 1976, Sciaky *et al.* 1978). Between these two
groups there is very little plasmid homology (Table 9.2). Hybridization
studies indicate homologies less than 30% while restriction endonuclease
patterns show no similarity with the exception of one 4 megadalton *Sma* I
fragment. However, the little homology which does exist between the two
groups is located at discrete regions of the plasmid (Hepburn & Hindley
1979; Fig. 9.4).

Table 9.2   Relationships between the plasmids from octopine- and nopaline-utilizing strains
of *Agrobacterium tumefaciens.*

Strain	Plasmid size (megadaltons)	Utilization of		%plasmid homology with DNA of	
		nopaline	octopine	strain A6	strain C58
C58	120	+	-	12	100
0362	149	+	-	16	93
181	158	+	-	12	73
IIBV7	118	+	-	28	27
A6	113	-	+	100	15
B2A	107	-	+	100	16
B6-806	125	-	+	89	16
15955	118	-	+	92	12

Incorporation of Plasmid DNA into Plant Cells

A complete Ti plasmid has not been detected in crown gall DNA but
fragments of the plasmid have (Chilton *et al.* 1978). The approach used
was to measure the reassociation of small amounts of single-stranded
radioactive plasmid DNA (probe) in the presence and absence of very large
amounts of tumour DNA (driver). If plasmid DNA sequences are present

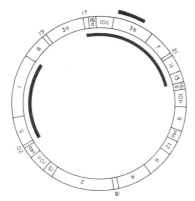

Fig. 9.4 Order of the 26 fragments produced by *Sma* I digestion of the plasmid from the octopine-utilizing strain B6-806 of *Agrobacter tumefaciens*. The solid lines within the map circle indicate the regions of homology between the octopine and nopaline types of plasmid. The extent of plasmid transcription in tumour cells is shown by the line outside the circle.

in the tumour DNA then the concentration of the probe is increased in the presence of tumour DNA and the probe DNA will reassociate more rapidly. The kinetics of reassociation depend both on the number of copies of the plasmid DNA sequences present in the tumour and on the fraction of the plasmid which is present.

Whole plasmid DNA renatured slightly faster in the presence of tumour DNA than in the presence of control DNAs. Treatment of tumour DNA with DNase abolished the acceleration. The data was consistent with the presence of one copy of the whole plasmid per ten diploid tumour cells or with multiple copies of a small part of the plasmid. In order to distinguish these possibilities the plasmid was digested with endonuclease *Sma* I into 26 fragments (Fig. 9.4) and each fragment hybridized with tumour DNA. Kinetic analysis showed that 20% of fragment 10c and 40% of fragment 3b hybridized and that there were 18 copies of fragment 3b per cell. What these studies did not and could not show was the location of the plasmid DNA fragments (T-DNA), whether the T-DNA is covalently bound to plant DNA and whether the 18 copies are dispersed.

^{32}P-pulse-labelled RNA from tumour cells, hybridized specifically to fragment 3b but not with 10c or any other *Sma* I generated fragments. Nor did RNA from normal cells bind to any fragment of the plasmid (Drummond *et al.* 1977). Oddly enough, cRNA synthesized from the whole Ti plasmid genome by *E. coli* RNA polymerase hybridized to fragments 10c and 3b as well as to fragments 1 and 5. It can be seen from Fig. 9.4 that these fragments correspond to the regions of homology between octopine and nopaline type plasmids. The significance of this latter observation is not clear.

The only plasmid encoded function so far detected in tumour cells is octopine or nopaline synthesis. Since the RNA transcript which hybridizes to fragment 3b was derived from an octopine-containing tumour it could carry the information for octopine biosynthesis. More positive evidence for this is given by the observation that a tumour line which had lost the ability to synthesize octopine contained plasmid sequences solely derived from fragment 10c.

The Potential of the Ti Plasmid as a Vector

As with CaMV, we do not have sufficient information about the role of fragments 3b and 10c to assess realistically the potential of the Ti plasmid. We know that the synthesis of octopine and nopaline is Ti-plasmid specific and we have speculated that fragment 3b may carry the requisite genetic information. Since tumours exist which do not synthesize octopine or nopaline it may be possible to replace fragment 3b with exogenous DNA. The problems of cloning DNA in large molecules like the Ti-plasmids could well be enormous but the advances made in recent years in our understanding of the mechanism of tumour induction suggest that these problems are not insurmountable. However, successful cloning of exogenous DNA in plant cells will require a much more detailed knowledge of the structure of fragment DNA, the mechanism whereby T-DNA is maintained in tumour cells and the control of transcription of T-DNA.

CONCLUDING REMARKS

Both CaMV and the Ti-plasmid have advantages and disadvantages as cloning vectors. CaMV-DNA is a convenient size for cloning but the DNA is not passed from one plant generation to the next. The Ti-plasmid is very large and not nearly as easy to handle as CaMV-DNA. However, the T-DNA is permanently maintained in tumour cells and plants derived from nopaline-containing tumour callus also contain nopaline. As to the future, it would be foolish to speculate about the advances that will be made in this area in the next five years. All we can hope is that you, the reader, will have obtained sufficient background information from the foregoing to enable you to appreciate these advances.

Chapter 10. Implications of Recombinant DNA Research

To date, the greatest contribution made by recombinant DNA research has undoubtedly been within molecular biology itself. In combination with Southern blot-transfer hybridization and rapid nucleotide sequencing, recombinant DNA technology has made possible the detailed structural analysis of a potentially very large number of eukaryotic genes. Those curious enough to read this book will probably know of the recent advances in our understanding of gene structure and will be aware of the importance of such knowledge. It is with eukaryotes that the challenge has been greatest, because of their large genomes, but the contribution of recombinant DNA research to prokaryote molecular biology must not be underestimated. The aim, of course, is to relate gene structure and function, first by comparison of known sequences, then either by introducing manipulated genes back into eukaryotic cells or by transcription *in vitro*. With these and possibly new ways of analysing this relationship, structural studies will certainly remain a major application of recombinant DNA research for many years to come.

Apart from application to direct structural investigations, molecular cloning provides DNAs of absolute sequence purity for application as hybridization probes in many other areas of molecular biology. Also within molecular biology, we have seen how bacterial genes encoding enzymes which are used in nucleic acid biochemistry, e.g. *E. coli* DNA ligase, can be manipulated so as to increase the yield of enzyme and make purification easier (see Chapters 4 and 6).

We who advocate recombinant DNA research have been eager to point out that not only is it a powerful tool for studying how genes work, but that it also can be applied to the commercial production of insulin, growth hormone, human interferon and other medically or industrially useful proteins. The work of Itakura *et al.* (1977) (see Chapter 3) on somatostatin, a hormone that inhibits the secretion of pituitary growth hormone, is an important step in this direction. The researchers who first isolated somatostatin required nearly half a million sheep brains to produce 5mg of the substance. Using the chemically-synthesized gene, 9 l of bacterial culture costing just a few dollars, produced the same amount. The relatively inexpensive commercial production of these proteins by fermentation depends upon efficient expression of cloned DNAs in suitable host microorganisms such as yeast or *E. coli.* However, we know that the factors affecting expression of heterologous genes are complex, and it is clear that maximizing expression of stable, cloned sequences is an area for continued research.

The ability to propagate recombinants between DNA sequences of species as diverse as man and bacteria has, however, engendered concern that researchers might inadvertently allow bacteria bearing new or unusual genetic combinations to escape from the laboratory and adversely affect human, animal or plant populations. Few scientific techniques have provoked as much speculation and conjecture about their potential for evil or good. As Arthur Kornberg (1974) has put it, 'Most people do not distinguish an atom from a molecule, a virus from a cell, or a cell from an organism; and so, through lack of understanding, may also be fearful about genetic chemistry. They might even want to enact laws which will regulate genetic research deemed to have a harmful *potential*'.

While much of the fear no doubt has been quite unfounded, concern was aroused initially among scientists involved in the research, and only later became a public issue. Table 10.1 gives the chronology of some of the early events in this story. An outcome of this concern was the establishment of a series of committees, in Britain and elsewhere, that have formulated research guidelines which have the force of law.

The UK and US guidelines categorize individual gene manipulation experiments according to the degree of physical and biological containment deemed appropriate. The aim of physical containment is to isolate the experiment so that the chance of organisms escaping from the laboratory is reduced or eliminated. This is simple in principle, but high containment is difficult to achieve in recombinant DNA research with its combination of microbiological and biochemical techniques. It also raises an issue that is peculiar to living biological hazards and for which experience with dangerous chemicals gives no precedent. With chemical hazards there is a more or less defined dose-response curve, but with a living bacterium or virus, the escape of a single agent which can multiply in the environment can lead to the same result as the escape of a much larger number. The value of partial containment is then called into question. Physical containment is therefore allied with biological containment, which aims to limit the ability of recombinants to survive or exchange genetic material in the environment beyond the laboratory.

The use of *E. coli* in recombinant DNA research has incited comment because it is a natural symbiont of man, primarily colonizing the gut. There might, therefore, be a real possibility that research workers themselves could provide a route for the escape of recombinants. In addition, and this was an issue raised when concern about gene manipulation was first voiced, the use of many of the common plasmid vectors which carry drug resistance markers could contribute to the persistence of recombinants in individuals

Table 10.1 Chronology of early events in the regulation of gene manipulation experiments.

United States of America

June 1973	Gordon Conference on Nucleic Acids - concern and debate about hazards of gene manipulation.
Sept. 1973	M. Singer and D. Soll, co-chairman of Gordon Conference publish letter (*Science* **181**, 1114) urging establishment of study group.
July 1974	'Berg letter' published (*Science* **185**, 303) reporting on National Academy of Science study group. Calls for moratorium on certain experiments.
Oct. 1974	NIH Committee established to formulate guidelines.
Feb. 1975	Meeting at Asilomar as recommended by NAS. Group organized by P. Berg, S. Brenner, D. Baltimore, R. Roblin and M. Singer recommends general guidelines (*Nature* **255**, 442). Many experiments remain 'deferred'. NIH Committee meeting follows.
June 1976	After much activity and controversy NIH Guidelines published. More detailed than Asilomar. Containment categories proposed. Emphasis on biological containment.

United Kingdom

July 1974	Following U.S. lead, Research Councils establish Ashby working party.
Dec. 1974	Ashby reports. Recommends Advisory Panel. Code of Practice said to be required.
Aug. 1975	Following Ashby recommendation, Williams Working Party appointed.
Aug. 1976	Williams Report and Health and Safety Commission Document published simultaneously. Williams recommends establishment of Genetic Manipulation Advisory Group (GMAG) and proposes containment categories. Emphasis on physical containment. HSC proposes very broad definition of experiments to be controlled.
Dec. 1976	GMAG meets. HSC definition restricted. Follows Willams' categories.

treated with antibiotics or in the natural environment where antibiotics are present through their use in animal husbandry, etc. Indeed one prominent researcher has commented that 'the world is a dilute solution of tetracycline'.

Bacteria other than *E. coli* can be used as host organisms, e.g. *B. subtilis* (see Chapter 3), but the advantages of working with the most fully characterized genetic system are overwhelming. The favoured strains for molecular biology are derivatives of *E. coli* K12, and it is fortunate that this strain does not grow well in the gut of man. It appears to require a higher partial pressure of oxygen than is found there. In one study (Petrocheilou & Richmond 1977), faeces of laboratory workers who handled nalidixic acid-resistant *E. coli* K12 and plasmids with multiple drug resistance markers were monitored every two or three days over a period of two years. Neither the K12 bacteria nor any of these plasmids were ever found in the faeces. Since these plasmids were proficient in conjugal transfer and the work was carried out without special precautions, one may conclude that there is not likely to be much risk of transmission of recombinant DNA when cloned in the currently used transfer-deficient plasmids or in *E. coli* K12 hosts.

While this evidence is reassuring to those actively engaged in gene manipulation experiments with *E. coli,* considerable effort has been put into developing attenuated or 'crippled' strains of *E. coli* K12 that incorporate a higher degree of biological containment. Thus, Curtiss (1976) and his associates have developed a strain, *E. coli* χ1776, that among other features, is multiply auxotrophic, is resistant to many phages, and is particularly sensitive to detergents and bile salts. Unfortunately, it has been found in practice that the incorporation of such attenuating properties frequently results in bacteria that grow poorly even at best, and have a poor transformation efficiency. Here is another area for continued research.

Today are we any nearer answering the question asked by the public? Are these new genetic combinations dangerous? In reply it must be said that it is of course possible to envisage gene manipulation experiments that *are* dangerous. For instance, incorporating the gene for a potent bacterial toxin into *E. coli* and then amplifying the toxin in large-scale culture would clearly be a hazardous procedure, but importantly, there is no reason to expect that on a global scale the novel bacterium would be any more pathogenic than pre-existing organisms. Pathogenicity depends upon many factors in which the new strain would be unlikely to excel.

In certain circumstances naked DNA can be an infectious or transforming agent. With DNA in general this is of no concern to us; we do not jib at eating a raw salad! However, gene manipulation does provide the means for preparing large amounts of DNA sequences derived from mammalian viruses and experiments have been devised to test the infectivity of viral DNA that has been covalently linked to a vector molecule and propagated in *E. coli* (Chan *et al.* 1979, Fried *et al.* 1979, Israel *et al.* 1979). These experiments, part of risk-assessing programmes and carried out under appropriately high containment according to existing regulations, involved inserting mouse polyoma virus DNA into phage λ derivatives or pBR322. Various recombinant molecules werc prepared and tested in mice or cultured mouse cells. It was found consistently that recombinants containing single copies of polyoma DNA were not biologically active in these tests unless the polyoma DNA was excised by cleavage with restriction endonuclease. This led to an infectivity similar to that of a molar equivalent of linearized polyoma DNA. The only recombinant DNAs that were active as entire molecules were those containing dimeric polyoma DNA inserts. Their activity was comparable with a molar equivalent of intact polyoma DNA that had been extracted from infected mouse cells. One conclusion that can be drawn from these experiments is that the potential for infectivity or tumorigenicity does persist when mammalian virus DNA is cloned in bacteria, and so there is a possibility that a library of clones obtained in a mammalian shot-gun experiment may contain potentially harmful sequences. Although it is unlikely that these cloned sequences pose any greater threat than the virus particles that can be released by cells in culture, research guidelines place considerable emphasis upon the identification and characterization of clones isolated in shot-gun experiments (see Chapter 6).

After the years of controversy there appears to be a welcome acceptance that gene manipulation experiments, of the kind described as detailed examples in preceding chapters, entail little danger beyond conventional microbiological research. Now it is to be hoped that research guidelines will evolve that are both rational and internationally consistent. The prospect for recombinant DNA research is very exciting. Some areas for future research have been mentioned already. Longer-term predictions might appear extravagant, but whilst it is clear that the cure of genetic diseases in man by gene treatment is not at hand there *is* great scope for application to crop-plant improvement, possibly using the vectors discussed in Chapter 9. In addition, future development of methods for the rapid chemical synthesis of defined DNA sequences has immense possibilities. Once the complex rules governing protein folding and enzyme catalysis are known sufficiently well to permit prediction, then we can say that genetic engineering, rather than mere manipulation, has truly come of age.

Appendix I Enzymes Used in Gene Manipulation

Enzyme	Uses	For example see page:
DNA polymerase I of *E. coli* (DNA-dependent DNA polymerase)	(1) Converting single-stranded DNA to double-stranded form, e.g. converting single-stranded tails on restriction fragments to blunt (flush) ends, or converting single-stranded cDNA to duplex cDNA. The DNA polymerase I molecule is susceptible to protease action such that it specifically splits into two fragments. The larger of these two fragments has polymerase and $3' \rightarrow 5'$ exonuclease activity but lacks $5' \rightarrow 3'$ exonuclease activity, and is sometimes employed instead of intact enzyme for this use	34
	(2) Nick-translation of DNA to prepare radioactive hybridization probes	68
Reverse transcriptase	(1) Synthesizing cDNA upon mRNA template, i.e. single-stranded DNA complementary to mRNA	23
	(2) Conversion of single-stranded cDNA to double-stranded form (alternative to DNA polymerase I)	—
RNA polymerase (DNA-dependent RNA polymerase)	(1) Making radioactive RNA copy of double-stranded DNA for use as a hybridization probe	—
	(2) Occasionally used to protect a promoter from endonuclease cleavage	36
Terminal Transferase (calf-thymus terminal deoxy-nucleotidyl transferase)	(1) Addition of oligodeoxynucleotide tails, e.g. oligo (dT), to $3'$-ends of DNA duplexes	80
DNA ligase	(1) Sealing single-strand nicks in DNA duplexes, e.g. those remaining when two *Eco* RI-generated fragments associate	75
	(2) (T4 DNA ligase only) Covalent linking of flush-ended DNA duplexes	36
Restriction endonucleases (type II only)	(1) Cleavage of DNA duplexes at defined sequences	79

Enzyme	Uses	For example see page:
DNase I	(1) Very limited treatment of double-stranded DNA so as to introduce nicks for nick-translation reactions	67
Nuclease S1	(1) Destroying single-stranded nucleic acid, e.g. converting cohesive ends of duplex DNA to flush ends, or trimming away single-stranded ends after conversion of single-stranded cDNA to double-stranded form	76
	(2) Cleavage of duplex DNA at A·T rich sequences following partial thermal denaturation	96
λ exonuclease	(1) Removing nucleotides from the 5′-ends of duplex DNA, usually to create an improved substrate for terminal transferase	21
Exonuclease III	(1) Removing nucleotides from the 3′-ends of duplex DNA	84 (Fig. 7.9)
Polynucleotide kinase	Labelling of 5′ ends of polynucleotides by transfer of γ-^{32}P from ATP	105

Appendix II As We Go
to Press ....

1. In a superb article entitled 'Restriction endonucleases, Simian Virus 40, and the new genetics' (*Science* **206**, 903-9) Nathans provides a detailed account of the way in which the techniques of gene manipulation have been used to dissect the SV40 genome. The material provided in this review not only complements the information on the biology of SV40 presented in Chapter 8, but also shows how techniques described in this book can be used to answer fundamental biological questions.

2. In an article entitled 'Trans-complementable copy-number mutants of plasmid Col E1' (*Nature,* in press) Twigg & Sherratt describe a derivative of pBR322, called pAT153, which now is being used widely as a cloning vehicle. Twigg & Sherratt observed that when a particular *Hae*II fragment was removed from Col E1 the plasmid copy number in *E. coli* increased 5 to 7-fold. The corresponding *Hae*II fragment was removed from pBR322 to produce pAT153. Cells containing pAT153 only have a 1.5 to 3-fold increased plasmid content compared to those containing pBR322. Although this increase is smaller than for the Col E1 deletion derivatives, pAT153 is still a useful cloning vector because of greater levels of plasmid and plasmid-specified gene products. In terms of biological containment pAT153 has a great advantage over pBR322. Although pBR322 is not self-transmissible, it can be mobilized at a frequency of 10^{-1} from cells containing a conjugative plasmid plus plasmid ColK. However, the *Hae*II fragment removed from pBR322 during the formation of pAT153 contains a DNA sequence essential for conjugal transfer. As a consequence pAT153 cannot be mobilized thus providing increased biological containment.

3. *'Northern' blotting.* Recently, a technique for transferring electrophoretically separated bands of *RNA* from an agarose gel to paper, has become widely used (Alwine J. C. *et al.* (1977) *Proc. Natn. Acad. Sci. U.S.A.* **74**, 5350-4). It is complementary to the blotting technique devised by Southern for the transfer of *DNA* to nitrocellulose sheets (see p. 7) and so has acquired the jargon term 'Northern' blotting!

Unlike single-stranded DNA, RNA does not bind tightly to nitrocellulose. Alwine *et al.* therefore adopted a procedure in which RNA bands are blot-transferred from the gel onto chemically reactive paper where it is bound covalently. The reactive paper is prepared by diazotization of aminobenzyl-oxymethyl-paper which itself can be prepared from Whatman 540 paper by a series of uncomplicated reactions. Once covalently bound, the RNA is available for hybridization with radiolabelled DNA probes. Hybridizing bands are located by autoradiography.

Because of the firm covalent binding of the RNA to the paper, such blot-transfers are reusable; the probe from previous hybridization reactions having been eluted by washing at a temperature at which hybrids are not stable. Although originally devised for the transfer of RNA bands, the chemically reactive paper is equally effective in binding denatured DNA. Indeed, small DNA fragments are more efficiently transferred to the diazotized paper derivative than to nitrocellulose, so that with the advantage of reusability this technique has won favour over the use of nitrocellulose in Southern blots.

Glossary

In addition to the terms defined here, many others are listed in the index and explained in the text.

Active site   The region of a protein molecule at which direct interaction with a substrate or regulatory molecule takes place.

Amber mutation   A class of suppressible mutations. An amber mutation results in the creation of a UAG codon in messenger RNA. UAG normally signifies translational termination, so that polypeptide synthesis stops at the amber site. However, such mutations can be suppressed in certain strains of *E. coli* possessing a tRNA with the AUC anticodon, hence inserting an amino-acid at the UAG site and permitting continued translation.

Antigen   A molecule that is capable of stimulating the production of neutralizing antibody proteins when injected into a vertebrate.

Anti-terminator   A protein which allows RNA polymerase to ignore transcriptional stop signals at particular sites in DNA.

Autoradiography   A technique for the detection of radioactively labelled molecules by overlaying the specimen with photographic film. When the film is developed an image is produced which corresponds to the location of the radioactivity.

Bacteriocin   Many bacterial strains liberate proteinaceous toxins called bacteriocins which are active only against closely related strains. Toxins of this type produced by *E. coli* are called *colicins.* Several different types have been isolated which kill sensitive cells by different mechanisms. *E. coli* cells are generally immune to the colicins which they produce.

Capped 5′-ends   The 5′-ends of eukaryotic mRNAs are modified post-transcriptionally to form ends with the general structure

$$m^7G(5′)ppp(5′)Nmp.....$$

where m^7G represents a 7-methyl-guanosine residue, and Nm a 2′-0-methylated nucleoside.

Capsid   The external protein shell or coat of a virus particle.

Catabolite repression   Decreased activity of many bacterial operons (e.g. the *lac* operon of *E. coli*) in the presence of glucose. Active catabolism of the glucose leads to a reduction in the intracellular concentration of cyclic AMP, thereby blocking an essential positive control signal for expression of glucose-sensitive operons.

Concatemer   A DNA structure made up of linearly repeated unit-length DNA molecules.

Colicin   *see* Bacteriocin.

Hairpin loop   A region of double helix formed by base-pairing within a single strand of DNA or RNA which has folded back on itself.

Heteroduplex   A DNA molecule formed by base-pairing between two strands that do not have completely complementary nucleotide sequences.

Heteroimmune   Two phages are heteroimmune if each is sensitive to its own repressor but not to that of the other.

Induction   1.(of an inducible enzyme). Increase in the rate of synthesis of an enzyme in response to the presence of a small molecule—an inducer. 2. (of a lysogen). Experimental elicitation of phage development from a prophage.

Lambda (λ) λgal—a transducing phage in which bacterial *gal* gene(s) have been incorporated in the genome of phage λ.

λgt.λB—a replacement vector derivative of λ in which the B fragment is replaceable by foreign DNA.   The letters gt signify that such a derivative can act as a generalized transducing phage through the incorporation of bacterial genes by manipulation *in vitro*.

λ *plac*—a transducing phage in which bacterial *lac* gene(s) have been incorporated in the genome of phage λ. λ *plac* stocks usually have 5 *Eco*R1 sites and are sometimes known as λ*plac* 5.   Derivatives have been constructed which have only 1 *Eco*R1 site and these are known as λ*plac* 5.1.

Lysogen   A bacterium that possesses a largely inactive phage genome and transmits it to its progeny.   Within a lysogen, expression of the phage genome is repressed owing to the action of a phage-specific repressor protein.

Operator   A site on a DNA molecule at which a specific repressor protein binds, hence regulating the expression of associated genes within the operon.

Operon   Two or more contiguous genes subject to coordinate regulation by an operator and repressor.

Papovaviruses   A group of animal viruses (*pa*pilloma, *po*lyoma and *va*cuolating viruses) with small circular duplex DNA genomes.

Probe (hybridization)   DNA or RNA molecule radiolabelled to a high specific radioactivity, used to detect the presence of a complementary sequence by molecular hybridization.

Promoter   Region of a DNA molecule at which RNA polymerase binds and initiates transcription.

Prophage   The state of a phage genome in a lysogen.

Retrovirus   Oncogenic RNA-containing virus which replicates through a DNA intermediate necessitating the presence of an RNA dependent DNA polymerase, i.e. reverse transcriptase.

Rho (ρ) factor   An *E. coli* protein involved in terminating transcription at certain DNA sites. See also 'anti-terminator'.

Temperature-sensitive mutation   Mutation leading to a gene product that is functional at low (high) temperature, but is inactive at a higher (lower) temperature.

Thermo-inducible   A thermo-inducible lysogen contains a prophage whose repressor is temperature-sensitive.   Raising the temperature leads to induction.

Transduction   Transfer of bacterial genes from one bacterium to another by a phage particle.

Transposon   A DNA element which can insert at random into plasmids or the bacterial chromosome independently of the host cell recombination system.   In addition to genes involved in insertion, transposons carry genes conferring new phenotypes on the host cell, e.g. kanamycin resistance, ampicillin resistance, etc.

References

Aaij C. & Borst P. (1972) The gel electrophoresis of DNA. *Biochim. biophys. Acta,* **269**, 192-200.

Abel P. & Trautner T. A. (1964) Formation of an animal virus within a bacterium. *Z. Vererb-Lehre,* **95**, 66-72.

Air G. M. (1979) Rapid DNA sequence analysis. *Crit. Rev. Biochem.,* **6**, 1-33.

Backmann K., Ptashne M. & Gilbert W. (1976) Construction of plasmids carrying the cI gene of bacteriophage λ. *Proc. natn. Acad. Sci. U.S.A.,* **73**, 4174-8.

Barnes W. M. (1977) Plasmid detection and sizing in single colony lysates. *Science,* **195**, 393-4.

Barnes W. M. (1979) Construction of an M13 histidine-transducing phage: a single-stranded cloning vehicle with one *Eco* RI site. *Gene,* **5**, 127-39.

Beggs J. D. (1978) Transformation of yeast by a replicating hybrid plasmid. *Nature,* **275**, 104-9.

Benton W. D. & Davis R. W. (1977) Screening λgt recombinant clones by hybridization to single plaques *in situ. Science,* **196**, 180-2.

Benzinger R., Enquist L. W. & Skalka A. (1975) Transfection of *Escherichia coli* sphaeroplasts. V. Activity of *rec*BC nuclease in *rec*⁺ and *rec*⁻ sphaeroplasts measured with different forms of bacteriophage DNA. *J. Virol.,* **15**, 861-71.

Bickle T. A., Brack C. & Yuan R. (1978) ATP-induced conformational changes in restriction endonuclease from *Escherichia coli* K12. *Proc. natn. Acad. Sci. U.S.A.,* **75**, 3099-103.

Blattner F. R., Williams B. G., Blechl A. E., Denniston-Thompson K., Faber H. E., Furlong L. A., Grunwald D. J., Kiefer D. O., Moore D. D., Schumm J. W., Sheldon E. L. & Smithies O. (1977) Charon phages: safer derivatives of bacteriophage lambda for DNA cloning. *Science,* **196**, 161-9.

Blobel G. & Dobberstein B. (1975) Transfer of proteins across membranes. I. Presence of proteolytically processed and unprocessed nascent immunoglobulin light chains on membrane-bound ribosomes of murine myeloma. *J. Cell Biol.,* **67**, 835-51.

Bolivar F. (1978) Construction and characterization of new cloning vehicles III. Derivatives of plasmid pBR322 carrying unique *Eco* RI sites for selection of *Eco* RI generated recombinant DNA molecules. *Gene,* **4**, 121-36.

Bolivar F., Rodriguez R. L., Betlach M. C. & Boyer H. W. (1977a) Construction and characterization of new cloning vehicles. I. Ampicillin-resistant derivatives of the plasmid pMB9. *Gene,* **2**, 75-93.

Bolivar F., Rodriguez R. L., Greene P. J., Betlach M. V., Heynecker H. L., Boyer H. W., Crosa J. H. & Falkow S. (1977b) Construction and characterization of new cloning vehicles. II. A multipurpose cloning system. *Gene,* **2**, 95-113.

Bomhoff G. H., Klapwijk F. M., Kester H. C. M., Schilperoort R. A., Hernalsteens J. P. & Schell J. (1976) Octopine and nopaline synthesis and breakdown genetically controlled by a plasmid of *Agrobacterium tumefaciens. Molec. gen. Genet.,* **145**, 177-81.

Braun A. C. & Stonier R. (1958) Morphology and physiology of plant tumours. *Protoplasmatologia,* **10**, 1-93.

Broome S. & Gilbert W. (1978) Immunological screening method to detect specific translation products. *Proc. natn. Acad. Sci. U.S.A.,* **75**, 2746-9.

Burrell C. J., Mackay P., Greenaway P. J., Hofschneider P. H. & Murray K. (1979) Expression in *Escherichia coli* of hepatitis B virus DNA sequences cloned in plasmid pBR322. *Nature,* **279**, 43-7.

Cameron J. R., Panasenko S. M., Lehman I. R. & Davis R. W. (1975) *In vitro* construction of bacteriophage λ carrying segments of the *Escherichia coli* chromosome: selection of hybrids containing the gene for DNA ligase. *Proc. natn. Acad. Sci. U.S.A.,* **72**, 3416-20.

Carlton B. C. & Helinski D. R. (1969) Heterogeneous circular DNA elements in vegetative cultures of *Bacillus megaterium. Proc. natn. Acad. Sci. U.S.A.,* **64**, 592-9.

Chan H. W., Israel M. A., Garon C. F., Rowe W. P. & Martin M. A. (1979) Molecular cloning of polyoma-virus DNA in *Escherichia coli* lambda phage vector system. *Science,* **203**, 887-92.

Chang A. C. Y. & Cohen S. N. (1974) Genome construction between bacterial species *in vitro:* replication and expression of *Staphylococcus* plasmid genes in *Escherichia coli. Proc. natn. Acad. Sci. U.S.A.,* **71**, 1030-4.

Chang A. C. Y., Nunberg J. H., Kaufman R. K., Ehrlich H. A., Schimke R. T. & Cohen S. N. (1978) Phenotypic expression in *E. coli* of a DNA sequence coding for mouse dihydrofolate reductase. *Nature,* **275**, 617-24.

Chang L. M. S. & Bollum F. J. (1971) Enzymatic synthesis of oligodeoxynucleotides. *Biochemistry,* **10**, 536-42.

Chang S. & Cohen S. N. (1977) *In vivo* site-specific genetic recombination promoted by the *Eco* RI restriction endonuclease. *Proc. natn. Acad. Sci. U.S.A.,* **74**, 4811-15.

Charnay P., Louise A., Fritsch A., Perrin D. & Tiollais P. (1979) Bacteriophage lambda *Escherichia coli* K12 vector host system for gene cloning and expression under lactose promoter control. II. DNA fragment insertion at the vicinity of the *lac* UV5 promoter. *Molec. gen. Genet.,* **170**, 171-8.

Charnay P., Perricaudet M., Galibert F. & Tiollais P. (1978) Bacteriophage lambda and plasmid vectors, allowing fusion of cloned genes in each of the three translational phases. *Nucl. Acids Res.,* **5**, 4479-94

Chilton M. D., Montoya A. L., Merlo D. J., Drummond M. H., Nutter R., Gordon M. P., Nester E. W. & Sciaky D. (1978) Restriction endonuclease mapping of a plasmid that confers oncogenicity upon *Agrobacterium tumefaciens* strain B6-806. *Plasmid,* **1**, 254-69.

Cohen S. N., Chang A. C. Y. & Hsu L. (1972) Nonchromosomal antibiotic resistance in bacteria: genetic transformation of *Escherichia coli* by R-factor DNA. *Proc. natn. Acad. Sci. U.S.A.,* **69**, 2110-4.

Collins J. & Brüning H. J. (1978) Plasmids usable as gene-cloning vectors in an *in vitro* packaging by coliphage λ: 'cosmids'. *Gene,* **4**, 85-107.

Collins J. & Hohn B. (1979) Cosmids: a type of plasmid gene-cloning vector that is packageable *in vitro* in bacteriophage λ heads. *Proc. natn. Acad. Sci. U.S.A.,* **75**, 4242-6.

Colman A., Byers M. J., Primrose S. B. & Lyons A. (1978) Rapid purification of plasmid DNAs by hydroxyapatite chromatography. *Eur. J. Biochem.,* **91**, 303-10.

Cosloy S. D. & Oishi M. (1973) Genetic transformation in *Escherichia coli* K12. *Proc. natn. Acad. Sci. U.S.A.,* **70**, 84 7.

Currier T. C. & Nester E. W. (1976) Evidence for diverse types of large plasmids in tumor-inducing strains of *Agrobacterium. J. Bact.,* **126**, 157-65.

Curtiss R. (1976) Genetic manipulation of microorganisms: potential benefits and biohazards. *A. Rev. Microbiol.,* **30**, 507-33.

Doy C. H., Gresshoff P. M. & Rolfe B. G. (1973) Biological and molecular evidence for the transgenosis of genes from bacteria to plant cells. *Proc. natn. Acad. Sci. U.S.A.,* **70**, 723-6.

Drummond M. H., Gordon M. P., Nester E. W. & Chilton M. D. (1977) Foreign DNA of bacterial plasmid origin is transcribed in crown gall tumours. *Nature,* **269**, 535-6.

Dugaiczyk A., Boyer H. W. & Goodman H. M. (1975) Ligation of *Eco* RI endonuclease-generated DNA fragments into linear and circular structures. *J. Molec. Biol.,* **96**, 171-84.

Dussoix D. & Arber W. (1962) Host specificity of DNA produced by *Escherichia coli*. II. Control over acceptance of DNA from infecting phage λ. *J. Molec. Biol.,* **5**, 37-49.

Efstratiadis A., Kafatos F. C., Maxam A. M. & Maniatis T. (1976) Enzymatic *in vitro* synthesis of globin genes. *Cell,* **7**, 279-88.

Ehrlich H. A., Cohen S. N. & McDevitt H. O. (1978) A sensitive radioimmunoassay for detecting products translated from cloned DNA fragments. *Cell,* **13**, 681-9.

Ehrlich S. D. (1977) Replication and expression of plasmids from *Staphylococcus aureus* in *Bacillus subtilis*. *Proc. natn. Acad. Sci. U.S.A.,* **74**, 1680-2.

Ehrlich S. D. (1978) DNA cloning in *Bacillus subtilis*. *Proc. natn. Acad. Sci. U.S.A.,* **75**, 1433-6.

Ehrlich S. D., Jupp S., Niaudet B. & Goze A. (1978) *Bacillus subtilis* as a host for DNA cloning. In *Genetic Engineering,* eds Boyer H. W. & Nicosia S., pp. 25-32. Elsevier-North Holland, Amsterdam.

Emmons S. W., MacCosham V. & Baldwin R. L. (1975) Tandem genetic duplications in phage lambda. III. The frequency of duplication mutants in two derivatives of phage lambda is independent of known recombination systems. *J. Molec. Biol.,* **91**, 133-46.

Falkow S. (1975) *Infectious multiple drug resistance.* London, Pion.

Fiers W., Contreras R., Haegeman G., Rogiers R., Van De Voorde A., Van Heuverswyn H., Van Herreweghe J., Volckaert G. & Ysebaert M. (1978) Complete nucleotide sequence of SV40 DNA. *Nature,* **273**, 113-20.

Fried M., Klein B., Murray K., Greenaway P., Tooze J., Boll W. & Weissmann C. (1979) Infectivity in mouse fibroblasts of polyoma DNA integrated into plasmid pBR322 or lambdoid phage DNA. *Nature,* **279**, 811-16.

Goff S. P. & Berg P. (1976) Construction of hybrid viruses containing SV40 and λ phage DNA segments and their propagation in cultured monkey cells. *Cell,* **9**, 695-705.

Gordon M. P., Farrand S. K., Sciaky D., Montoya A. L., Chilton M. D., Merlo D. J. & Nester E. W. (1979) In *Molecular Biology of Plants, Symposium,* University of Minnesota, ed. Rubenstein I. Academic Press, London.

Gottesmann M. E. & Yarmolinsky M. D. (1968) The integration and excision of the bacteriophage lambda genome. *Cold Spring Harb. Symp. quant. Biol.,* **33**, 735-47.

Grunstein M. & Hogness D. S. (1975) Colony hybridization: a method for the isolation of cloned DNAs that contain a specific gene. *Proc. natn. Acad. Sci. U.S.A.,* **72**, 3961-5.

Gumport R. I. & Lehman I. R. (1971) Structure of the DNA ligase adenylate intermediate: lysine (ε-amino) linked AMP. *Proc. natn. Acad. Sci., U.S.A.,* **68**, 2559-63.

Hamer D. H. (1977) SV40 carrying an *Escherichia coli* suppressor gene. In *Recombinant Molecules: Impact on Science and Society,* eds. Beers R. G. & Bassett E. G., pp. 317-35. Raven, New York.

Hardies S. C. & Wells R. D. (1976) Preparative fractionation of DNA restriction fragments by reversed phase column chromatography. *Proc. natn. Acad. Sci. U.S.A.,* **73**, 3117-21.

Hepburn A. G. & Hindley J. (1979) Regions of DNA sequence homology between an octopine and a nopaline Ti plasmid of *Agrobacterium tumefaciens*. *Molec. gen. Genet.,* **169**, 163-72.

Hershfield V., Boyer H. W., Yanofsky C., Lovett M. A. & Helinski D. R. (1974) Plasmid ColE1 as a molecular vehicle for cloning and amplification of DNA. *Proc. natn. Acad. Sci. U.S.A.,* **71**, 3455-9.

Higuchi R., Paddock G. V., Wall R. & Salser W. (1976) A general method for cloning eukaryotic structural gene sequences. *Proc. natn. Acad. Sci. U.S.A.,* **73**, 3146-50.

Hinnen A., Hicks J. B. & Fink G. R. (1978) Transformation of yeast. *Proc. natn. Acad. Sci. U.S.A.,* **75**, 1929-33.

Hohn B. (1975) DNA as substrate for packaging into bacteriophage lambda, *in vitro*. *J. Molec. Biol.,* **98**, 93-106.

Hohn B. & Murray K. (1977) Packaging recombinant DNA molecules into bacteriophage particles *in vitro*. *Proc. natn. Acad. Sci. U.S.A.,* **74**, 3259-63.

Hopkins A. S., Murray N. E. & Brammar W. J. (1976) Characterization of λtrp-transducing bacteriophages made *in vitro*. *J. Molec. Biol.*, **107**, 549-69.

Horst J., Kluge F., Beyreuther K. & Gerok W. (1975) Gene transfer to human cells: transducing phage λp*lac* gene expression in Gm$_r$-gangliosidosis fibroblasts. *Proc. natn. Acad. Sci. U.S.A.*, **72**, 3531-5.

Howell S. H. & Hull R. (1978) Replication of cauliflower mosaic-virus and transcription of its genome in turnip leaf protoplasts. *Virology*, **86**, 468-81.

Hull R. & Howell S. H. (1978) Structure of cauliflower mosaic-virus genome. II. Variation in DNA-structure and sequence between isolates. *Virology*, **86**, 482-93.

Hull R. & Shepherd R. J. (1976) Coat proteins of cauliflower mosaic-virus. *Virology*, **70**, 217-20.

Hull R. & Shepherd R. J. (1977) Structure of cauliflower mosaic-virus genome. *Virology*, **79**, 216-30.

Humphries P., Old R., Coggins L. W., McShane T., Watson C. & Paul J. (1978) Recombinant plasmids containing *Xenopus laevis* structural genes derived from complementary DNA. *Nucl. Acids Res.*, **5**, 905-24.

Inouye H. & Beckwith J. (1977) Synthesis and processing of an *Escherichia coli* alkaline phosphatase precursor *in vitro*. *Proc. natn. Acad. Sci. U.S.A.*, **74**, 1440-4.

Israel M. A., Chan H. W., Rowe W. P. & Martin M. A. (1979) Molecular cloning of polyoma virus DNA in *Escherichia coli* plasmid vector system. *Science*, **203**, 883-7.

Itakura K., Hirose T., Crea R., Riggs A. D., Heyneker H. L., Bolivar F. & Boyer H. W. (1977) Expressions in *Escherichia coli* of a chemically synthesized gene for the hormone somatostatin. *Science*, **198**, 1056-63.

Jackson D. A., Symons R. H. & Berg P. (1972) Biochemical method for inserting new genetic information into DNA Simian Virus 40: circular SV40 DNA molecules containing lambda phage genes and the galactose operon of *Escherichia coli*. *Proc. natn. Acad. Sci. U.S.A.*, **69**, 2904-9.

Jacob A. E., Cresswell J. M., Hedges R. W., Coetzee J. N. & Beringer J. E. (1976) Properties of plasmids constructed by *in vitro* insertion of DNA from *Rhizobium leguminosarum* or *Proteus mirabilis* into RP4. *Molec. gen. Genet.*, **147**, 315-23.

Johnson C. B., Grierson D. & Smith H. (1973) Expression of λp*lac*5 DNA in cultured cells of a higher plant. *Nature, N. Biol.*, **244**, 105-7.

Johnson P. H. & Grossman L. I. (1977) Electrophoresis of DNA in agarose gels: optimizing separations of conformational isomers of double-stranded and single-stranded DNAs. *Biochemistry*, **16**, 4217-25.

Jones K. & Murray K. (1975) A procedure for detection of heterologous DNA sequences in lambdoid phage by *in situ* hybridization. *J. Molec. Biol.*, **51**, 393-409.

Kelly T. J. & Smith H. O. (1970) A restriction enzyme from *Hemophilus influenzae*. II. Base sequence of the recognition site. *J. Molec. Biol.*, **51**, 393-409.

Kleinhofs A., Eden F. C., Chilton M. D. & Bendich A. J. (1975) On the question of the integration of exogenous bacterial DNA into plant DNA. *Proc. natn. Acad. Sci. U.S.A.*, **72**, 2748-52.

Kornberg A. (1974) *DNA Synthesis*. Freeman & Co., San Francisco.

Kramer R. A., Cameron J. R. & Davis R. W. (1976) Isolation of bacteriophage λ containing yeast ribosomal RNA genes: screening by *in situ* RNA hybridization to plaques. *Cell*, **8**, 227-32.

Lawn R. M., Fritsch E. F., Parker R. C., Blake G. & Maniatis T. (1978) The isolation and characterization of linked δ and β-globin genes from a cloned library of human DNA. *Cell*, **15**, 1157-74.

Leder P., Tiemeier D. & Enquist L. (1977) EK2 derivatives of bacteriophage lambda useful in the cloning of DNA from higher organisms: the λgt WES system. *Science*, **196**, 175-7.

Lederberg S. & Meselson M. (1964) Degradation of non-replicating bacteriophage DNA in non-accepting cells. *J. Molec. Biol.*, **8**, 623-8.

Ledoux L. & Huart R. (1968) Integration and replication of DNA of *M. lysodeikticus* in DNA of germinating barley. *Nature, 218,* 1256-9.

Ledoux L., Huart R. & Jacobs M. (1971) Fate of exogenous DNA in *Arabidopsis thaliana:* translocation and integration. *Eur. J. Biochem., 23,* 96-108.

Le Hegarat J. C. & Anagnostopoulos C. (1977) Detection and characterization of naturally occurring plasmids in *Bacillus subtilis. Molec. gen. Genet., 157,* 167-174.

Lobban P. E. & Kaiser A. D. (1973) Enzymatic end-to-end joining of DNA molecules. *J. Molec. Biol., 78,* 453-71.

Lung M. C. Y. & Pirone T. P. (1974) Acquisition factor required for aphid transmission of purified cauliflower mosaic-virus. *Virology, 60,* 260-4.

Luria S. E., Darnell J. E., Baltimore D. & Campbell A. (1978) *General Virology,* 3e. John Wiley & Sons, New York.

Mandel M. & Higa A. (1970) Calcium-dependent bacteriophage DNA infection. *J. Molec. Biol., 53,* 159-62.

Maniatis T., Sim Gek Kee, Efstratiadis A. & Kafatos F. C. (1976) Amplification and characterization of a β-globin gene synthesized *in vitro. Cell, 8,* 163-82.

Meagher R. B., Shepherd R. J. & Boyer H. W. (1977) Structure of cauliflower mosaic-virus. I. Restriction endonuclease map of cauliflower mosaic-virus DNA. *Virology, 80,* 367-75.

Meagher R. B., Tait R. C., Betlach M. & Boyer H. W. (1977) Protein expression in *E. coli* minicells by recombinant plasmids. *Cell, 10,* 521-36.

Mercerau-Puijalon O., Royal A., Cami B., Garapin A., Krust A., Gannon F. & Kourilsky P. (1978) Synthesis of an ovalbumin-like protein by *Escherichia coli* K12 harbouring a recombinant plasmid. *Nature, 275,* 505-10.

Merril C. R., Geier M. R. & Petricciani J. C. (1971) Bacterial virus gene expression in human cells. *Nature, 233,* 398-400.

Mertz J. E. & Berg P. (1974) Defective simian virus 40 genomes. Isolation and growth of individual clones. *Virology, 62,* 112-24.

Meselson M. & Yuan R. (1968) DNA restriction enzyme from *E. coli. Nature, 217,* 1110-14.

Messing J., Gronenborn B., Muller-Hill B. & Hofschneider P. H. (1977) Filamentous coliphage M13 as a cloning vehicle: insertion of a *Hind* II fragment of the *lac* regulatory region in M13 replicative form *in vitro. Proc. natn. Acad. Sci. U.S.A., 74,* 3642-6.

Moir A. & Brammar W. J. (1976) Use of specialized transducing phages in amplification of enzyme production. *Molec. gen. Genet., 149,* 87-99.

Montoya A. L., Chilton M. D., Gordon M. P., Sciaky D. & Nester E. W. (1977) Octopine and nopaline metabolism in *Agrobacterium tumefaciens* and crown gall tumor cells: role of plasmid genes. *J. Bact., 129,* 101-7.

Morrow J. F., Cohen S. N., Chang A. C. Y., Boyer H. W., Goodman H. M. & Helling R. B. (1974) Replication and transcription of eukaryotic DNA in *Escherichia coli. Proc. natn. Acad. Sci. U.S.A., 71,* 1743-7.

Mulligan R. C., Howard B. H. & Berg P. (1979) Synthesis of rabbit β-globin in cultured monkey kidney cells following infection with SV40 β-globin recombinant genome. *Nature, 277,* 108-114.

Murray K. & Murray N. E. (1975) Phage lambda receptor chromosomes for DNA fragments made with restriction endonuclease III of *Haemophilus influenzae* and restriction endonuclease I of *Escherichia coli. J. Molec. Biol., 98,* 551-64.

Murray N. E., Batten P. L. & Murray K. (1973) Restriction of bacteriophage λ by *Escherichia coli* K. *J. Molec. Biol., 81,* 395-407.

Murray N. E., Brammar W. J. & Murray K. (1977) Lambdoid phages that simplify recovery of *in vitro* recombinants. *Molec. gen. Genet., 150,* 53-61.

Newman A. J., Linn T. G. & Hayward R. S. (1979) Evidence for cotranscription of the RNA polymerase genes RPOBC with a ribosome protein gene of *Escherichia coli. Molec. gen. Genet., 169,* 195-204.

Novick R. P., Clowes R. C., Cohen S. N., Curtiss R., Datta N. & Falkow S. (1976) Uniform nomenclature for bacterial plasmids: a proposal. *Bact. Rev.,* **40**, 168-89.

Ohsumi M., Vovis G. F. & Zinder N. D. (1978) Isolation and characterization of an *in vivo* recombinant between filamentous bacteriophage f1 and plasmid-PSC101. *Virology,* **89**, 438-49.

Olivera B. M., Hall Z. W. & Lehman I. R. (1968) Enzymatic joining of polynucleotides. V. A DNA adenylate intermediate in the polynucleotide joining reaction. *Proc. natn. Acad. Sci., U.S.,* **61**, 237-44.

Panasenko S. M., Cameron J. R., Davis R. W. & Lehman I. R. (1977) Five hundredfold overproduction of DNA ligase after induction of a hybrid lambda lysogen constructed *in vitro. Science,* **196**, 188-9.

Parkinson J. S. & Huskey R. J. (1971) Deletion mutants of bacteriophage lambda. I. Isolation and initial characterization. *J. Molec. Biol.,* **56**, 369-84.

Paterson B. M., Roberts B. E. & Kuff E. L. (1977) Structural gene identification and mapping by DNA.mRNA hybrid-arrested cell-free translation. *Proc. natn. Acad. Sci. U.S.A.,* **74**, 4370-4.

Petrocheilou V. & Richmond M. H. (1977) Absence of plasmid or *Escherichia coli* K-12 infection among laboratory personnel engaged in R-plasmid research. *Gene,* **2**, 323-7.

Primrose S. B. & Dimmock N. J. (1980) *Introduction to Modern Virology,* 2e. Blackwell Scientific Publications, Oxford.

Radloff R., Bauer W. & Vinograd J. (1967) A dye-buoyant-density method for the detection and isolation of closed circular duplex DNA: the closed circular DNA in HeLa cells. *Proc. natn. Acad. Sci. U.S.A.,* **57**, 1514-21.

Ratzkin B. & Carbon J. (1977) Functional expression of cloned yeast DNA in *Escherichia coli. Proc. natn. Acad. Sci. U.S.A.,* **74**, 487-91.

Reddy V. B., Thimmappaya B., Dhar R., Subramanian K. N., Zain B. S., Pan J., Ghosh P. K., Celma M. L. & Weissman S. M. (1978) The genome of simian virus 40. *Science,* **200**, 494-502.

Rigby P. W. J., Dieckmann M., Rhodes C. & Berg P. (1977) Labelling deoxyribonucleic acid to high specific activity *in vitro* by nick translation with DNA polymerase I. *J. Molec. Biol.,* **113**, 237-51.

Roberts R. J. (1978) Restriction and modification enzymes and their recognition sequences. *Gene,* **4**, 183-93.

Roberts T. M., Kacich R. & Ptashne M. (1979) A general method for maximizing the expression of a cloned gene. *Proc. natn. Acad. Sci. U.S.A.,* **76**, 760-4.

Rosamond J., Endlich B. & Linn S. (1979) Electron microscopic studies of the mechanism of action of the restriction endonuclease of *Escherichia coli* B. *J. Molec. Biol.,* **129**, 619-35.

Roychoudhury R., Jay E. & Wu R. (1976) Terminal labelling and addition of homopolymer tracts to duplex DNA fragments by terminal deoxynucleotidyl transferase. *Nucl. Acids Res.,* **3**, 863-77.

Scandella D. & Arber W. (1976) Phage λ DNA infection in *Escherichia coli* pel mutants is restored by mutations in phage genes V or H. *Virology,* **69**, 206-15.

Schell J. & Van Montagu M. (1977) The Ti-plasmid of *Agrobacterium tumefaciens,* a natural vector for the introduction of nif genes in plants. In *Genetic Engineering for Nitrogen Fixation,* ed. Hollaender A., pp. 159-79. Plenum Press, New York.

Scheller R. H., Dickerson R. E., Boyer H. W., Riggs A. D. & Itakura K. (1977) Chemical synthesis of restriction enzyme recognition sites useful for cloning. *Science,* **196**, 177-80.

Sciaky D., Montoya A. L. & Chilton M. D. (1978) Fingerprints of *Agrobacterium* Ti plasmids. *Plasmid,* **1**, 238-53.

Sgaramella V. (1972) Enzymatic oligomerization of bacteriophage P22 DNA and of linear Simian Virus 40 DNA. *Proc. natn. Acad. Sci. U.S.A.,* **69**, 3389-93.

Shepherd R. J. (1976) DNA viruses of higher plants. *Adv. Virus Res.,* **20**, 305-39.

Shine J. & Dalgarno L. (1975) Determinant of cistron specificity in bacterial ribosomes. *Nature,* **254,** 34-8.

Shine J., Seeburg P. H., Martial J. A., Baxter J. D. & Goodman H. M. (1977) Construction and analysis of recombinant DNA for human chorionic somatomammotropin. *Nature,* **270,** 494-9.

Shorenstein R. G. & Losick R. (1973) Comparative size and properties of the sigma subunits of ribonucleic acid polymerase from *Bacillus subtilis* and *Escherichia coli. J. biol. Chem.,* **248,** 6170-3.

Skalka A. & Shapiro L. (1976) *In situ* immunoassays for gene translation products in phage plaques and bacterial colonies. *Gene,* **1,** 65-79.

Smith D. F., Searle P. F. & Williams J. G. (1979) Characterization of bacterial clones containing DNA sequences derived from *Xenopus laevis. Nucl. Acids. Res.,* **6,** 487-506.

Smith H. O. & Nathans D. (1973) A suggested nomenclature for bacterial host modification and restriction systems and their enzymes. *J. Molec. Biol.,* **81,** 419-23.

Smith E. F. & Townsend C. O. (1907) A plant-tumour of bacterial origin. *Science,* **25,** 671-3.

Smith H. O. & Wilcox K. W. (1970) A restriction enzyme from *Hemophilus influenzae.* I. Purification and general properties. *J. Molec. Biol.,* **51,** 379-91.

Southern E. M. (1975) Detection of specific sequences among DNA fragments separated by gel electrophoresis. *J. Molec. Biol.,* **98,** 503-17.

Spoerel N., Herrlich P. & Bickle T. A. (1979) A novel bacteriophage defence mechanism: the anti-restriction protein. *Nature,* **278,** 30-4.

Stallcup M. R., Sharrock W. J. & Rabinowitz J. C. (1974) Ribosome and messenger specificity in protein synthesis by bacteria. *Biochem. biophys. Res. Commun.,* **58,** 92-8.

Steitz J. A. (1979) Genetic signals and nucleotide sequences in messenger RNA. In *Biological Regulation and Development. - 1. Gene Expression,* ed. Goldberger R. F., pp. 349-99. Plenum Press, New York.

Struhl K., Cameron J. R. & Davis R. W. (1976) Functional genetic expression of eukaryotic DNA in *Escherichia coli. Proc. natn. Acad. Sci. U.S.A.,* **73,** 1471-5.

Struhl K., Stinchcomb D. T., Scherer S. & Davis R. W. (1979) High-frequency transformation of yeast: autonomous replication of hybrid DNA molecules. *Proc. natn. Acad. Sci. U.S.A.,* **76,** 1035-9.

Szeto W., Hamer D. H., Carlson P. S. & Thomas C. A. (1977) Cloning of cauliflower mosaic virus (CLMV) DNA in *Escherichia coli. Science,* **196,** 210-12.

Telford J., Boseley P., Schaffner W. & Birnstiel M. (1977) Novel screening procedure for recombinant plasmids. *Science,* **195,** 391-3.

Thomas M., Cameron J. R. & Davis R. W. (1974) Viable molecular hybrids of bacteriophage lambda and eukaryotic DNA. *Proc. natn. Acad. Sci. U.S.A., 71, 4579-83.*

Thomas M., White R. L. & Davis R. W. (1976) Hybridization of RNA to double-stranded DNA: formation of R-loops. *Proc. natn. Acad. Sci. U.S.A.,* **73,** 2294-8.

Thorne H. V. (1966) Electrophoretic separation of polyoma virus DNA from host cell DNA. *Virology,* **29,** 234-9.

Thorne H. V. (1967) Electrophoretic characterization and fractionation of polyoma virus DNA. *J. Molec. Biol.,* **24,** 203-11.

Tikchonenko T. I., Karamov E. V., Zavizion B. A. & Naroditsky B. S. (1978) *Eco*RI* activity: enzyme modification or activation of accompanying endonuclease? *Gene,* **4,** 195-212.

Tilghman S. M., Tiemeier D. C., Polsky F., Edgell M. H., Seidman J. G., Leder A., Enquist L. W., Norman B. & Leder P. (1977) Cloning specific segments of the mammalian genome: bacteriophage λ containing mouse globin and surrounding gene sequences. *Proc. natn. Acad. Sci. U.S.A.,* **74,** 4406-10.

Van Larebeke N., Engler G., Holsters M., Van Den Elsacker S., Zaenen I., Schilperoort R. A. & Schell J. (1974) Large plasmid in *Agrobacterium tumefaciens* essential for crown gall-inducing ability. *Nature,* **252,** 169-70.

Vapnek D., Hautala J. A., Jacobson J. W., Giles N. H. & Kushner S. R. (1977) Expression in *Escherichia coli* K12 of the structural gene for catabolic dehydroquinase of *Neurospora crassa. Proc. natn. Acad. Sci. U.S.A.,* **74,** 3508-12.

Velten J., Fukada K. & Abelson J. (1976) *In vitro* construction of bacteriophage λ and plasmid DNA molecules containing DNA fragments from bacteriophage T4. *Gene,* **1,** 93-106.

Villa-Komaroff L., Efstratiadas A., Broome S., Lomedico P., Tizard R., Naber S. P., Chick W. L. & Gilbert W. (1978) A bacterial clone synthesizing proinsulin. *Proc. natn. Acad. Sci. U.SA.,* **75,** 3727-31.

Volvovitch M., Drugeon G. & Yot P. (1978) Studies on the single-stranded discontinuities of the cauliflower mosaic virus genome. *Nucl. Acids Res.,* **5,** 2913-25.

Watson B., Currier T. C., Gordon M. P., Chilton M. D. & Nester E. W. (1975) Plasmid required for virulence of *Agrobacterium tumefaciens. J. Bact.,* **123,** 255-64.

Wensink P. C., Finnegan D. J., Donelson J. E. & Hogness D. S. (1974) A system for mapping DNA sequences in the chromosomes of *Drosophila melanogaster. Cell,* **3,** 315-25.

White R. L. & Hogness D. S. (1977) R loop mapping of the 18S and 28S sequences in the long and short repeating units of *Drosophila melanogaster* rDNA. *Cell,* **10,** 177-92.

Wigler M., Sweet R., Sim G. K., Wold B., Pellicer A., Lacy E., Maniatis T. Silverstein S. & Axel R. (1979) Transformation of mammalian cells with genes from procaryotes and eucaryotes. *Cell,* **16,** 777-85.

Yang Chou J. & Martin R. G. (1974) Complementation analysis of Simian Virus 40 mutants. *J. Virol.,* **13,** 1101-9.

Zaenen I., Van Larebeke N., Teuchy H., Van Montagu M. & Schell J. (1974) Supercoiled circular DNA in crown-gall inducing *Agrobacterium* strains. *J. Molec. Biol.,* **86,** 109-127.

Index